TIES
THAT BIND

William Lyon Mackenzie King and Franklin Delano Roosevelt, at Quebec City, 1936.

TIES
THAT BIND

Canadian-American Relations in Wartime
From the Great War to the Cold War

R. D. Cuff

J. L. Granatstein

Second Edition

SAMUEL STEVENS
HAKKERT & COMPANY
TORONTO and SARASOTA
1977

Samuel Stevens Edition

Cloth: ISBN 0-89522-000-8
Paper: ISBN 0-89522-001-6

Hakkert Edition

Cloth: ISBN 0-88866-579-2
Paper: ISBN 0-88866-580-6

Library of Congress Catalogue Card Number 77-73816

Canadian Cataloguing in Publication Data

Cuff, Robert D., 1941-
   Ties that bind

First ed. published in 1975 under title: Canadian-
American relations in wartime.

Includes Index.
ISBN 0-88866-579-2 bd. ISBN 0-88866-580-6 pa.

1. Canada — Foreign relations — United States. 2.
United States — Foreign relations — Canada. I.
Granatstein, J.L., 1939-   II. Title. III. Title:
Canadian-American relations in wartime.

FC249.C83 1977   327.71'073   C77-001220-5
F1029.5.U6C83 1977

Design by Helmut Rath

Printed and bound in Canada.

Samuel Stevens & Company
Box 3899
Sarasota, Florida 33578

A. M. Hakkert Ltd.
554 Spadina Crescent
Toronto, Canada M5S 2J9

093711

CONTENTS

PREFACE

Studies of Canadian-American relations are one of the great staples of Canadian intellectual life, and a preoccupation with the unequal relationship of the Dominion and the Republic is, like saying "eh," one of the litmus tests of the true Canadian. But how the relationship is judged at any particular point in time seems to depend in part on the prevailing political mood, and perhaps this too easy catering to the vagaries of public feeling is responsible for the preponderance of cliches that still mark studies of the undefended border. These essays, of course, are also products of contemporary political and cultural concerns. No doubt they will reflect certain traits that such motivation inevitably seems to produce; ideally, they will offer something more as well.

We have focussed on war and cold war, and for good reason. The objective fact of war has played a particularly significant part in the evolution of Canadian-American relations, forcing adjustments and readjustments that often overrode the wishes of the political leaders. The periods of war in the twentieth century, we suggest, are even more important than the years of peace in understanding the factors that moulded and shaped the nature of our present.

These are the crisis points, the nodes, in the general evolution, for each war has raised into bold relief questions of identity, power and autonomy for both countries. For the United States, the Great War marked its emergence as a great power and the near capture of world financial hegemony, trends that were carried to completion from 1939 to 1945. For Canada, the 1914-18 war saw great leaps forward toward autonomy and industrialization, while the Second World War made the nation into a large industrial power and a leader of the "middle powers." The two world wars and the early years of the Cold War, as these essays will demonstrate, also forced Canadians and Americans to come to terms with each other in ways that neither, perhaps, had foreseen or wanted.

This is the theme of this book. Wars, both hot and cold, have forced new relationships on both countries, with profoundly important effects on the weaker of the two. Canadian prime ministers have had to deal with pressures of a new intensity and, some argue, they folded quickly under the strain and sold us out to the Americans. This is a proposition that today is common in both radical and conservative varieties of Canadian scholarship, and the Hyde Park Agreement of 1941, to cite an example, is sometimes seen as a classic example of Mackenzie King's failure to maintain Canadian interests in the face of encroachments from the south. To us, this seems a misreading of the evidence for a period that was marked by difficulties with foreign exchange and war exports and with extraordinary problems throughout the whole United States-United Kingdom-Canada nexus. Robert Borden, interestingly enough, had faced almost exactly the same kinds of pressures in 1917-18, and his government had been forced to seek similar relief from Washington.

The war prime ministers were not trying to bind Canada to the American chariot wheels. They did not consciously seek to reduce their freedom of manoeuvre or to weaken their capacity to initiate policy. On the contrary. They hoped to increase their freedom of action during a time of major change. A deal with the United States would expand Canada's markets and access to resources and exchange; it would keep Canadians working and producing; it would prevent the transfer of British orders from Canada to the United States; and if it came to that it would give Canada a better bargaining position with the British too.

Of course, intentions are not always the same as consequences. Nor is it always safe to read motivations from outcomes. In retrospect, it might appear that Canadian leaders like Borden, King and Pearson intended certain developments that have, in fact, limited Canadian independence. But this is not necessarily so, and indeed is extremely unlikely. Their policies, however, can be criticized without imputing disloyalty. To understand their actions is not necessarily to agree with them.

What happened during the war and cold war periods? These different yet similar crises force-fed striking readjustments in Canadian-American relationships, readjustments of a kind impossible to contemplate in the politics of peacetime. Structural changes were so great, in other words, that ideological conviction and established political patterns were often overridden. Thus it made little difference in 1917 that Borden had campaigned against reciprocity and for the national policy and the Empire in 1911. It made little difference that some Canadians and Englishmen hated to see Canada turn away from the City of London and to Wall Street and the American money markets in both wars. The needs of the hour demanded such action; the structural and institutional factors required it.

Among the institutional conditions of war in the twentieth century is an acceleration of those trends usually associated with bureaucratization. Modern warfare has encouraged the rationalization of collective activity. It has placed a premium on large-scale productive units. It has underscored the importance of long-range planning and administrative mechanisms. The war years demanded an increase in the number of administrative agreements binding the two North American economies together and, after the Second World War, these agreements proved far more durable than after 1918 primarily because the atmosphere of crisis continued and intensified. The wars also accelerated the flow of power to the central governments in both the U.S. and Canada, and increased the importance of and opportunity for executive agreements between them. The wars, in fact, raised again the constant question of Canadian life: why should Canada not be integrated into the United States?

Simultaneously and somewhat paradoxically, the wars had the effect of making Canadians conscious of their national identity. Canadian nationalism, we are told, was born on Vimy Ridge and tempered and refined in Normandy and on the Scheldt. The wars did increase the English-Canadian consciousness of separate identity, but the political leaders who nurtured and fostered this nationalism presided at the same time over the drafting of the economic agreements that linked Canadian economic well-being inextricably to that of the United States. Perhaps this is simply a reflection of the way Borden, King and Pearson separated politics and economics in their own minds. Perhaps too they sought to divert the public's attention to the intangibles while they struggled to stay upright as the military and economic ground shifted beneath their feet.

The same situation may exist today. The cultural nationalism of Canada is alive in a way that it never has been before, although the underlying military and economic patterns of Canadian-American relations have altered little in the postwar years. This has important implications for the contemporary debate. The problems of the present have roots in the past. Deep structural and historical conditions fix the parameters within which politicians play out their hands. Failure to appreciate these parameters raises a false sense of our freedom to alter them. Suggestions for change, in other words, have to bear some relationship to the potentiality for change. If a study of the past does not always provide a ready source of optimism about the hope for change today, it may make us freer tomorrow.

With two exceptions these essays are joint products. Chapter 1 was written by Cuff alone while Chapter 5 was written by Granatstein. We are grateful to the Canadian Historical Association for permitting us to reprint Chapter 1, which first appeared in *Historical Papers*, 1969; to the University of Toronto Press for permission to reprint Chapter 4, which first appeared in the *Canadian Historical Review*, 1974; to the *Canadian Review of American Studies*, 1974 for permission to reprint Chapter 5; and to the *Queen's Quarterly*, 1972, for permission to reprint Chapter 8. Chapter 6 is a much revised version of an article that first appeared in *Canadian Forum*, 1972, and we are grateful to Professor John English for challenging our first effort and forcing us to reconsider some of our arguments.

Finally our joint and separate researches have been greatly aided by the Canada Council and the York University Minor Research Fund. We are grateful too for research assistance provided by Stan Vittoz.

R.D.C.
J.L.G.

INTRODUCTION TO
THE SECOND EDITION

War has been a crucial factor in Canadian-American relations. In the 18th and 19th centuries, the Seven Years War, the American War of Independence, and the Civil War dramatically shaped the emergence of the Canadian nation; the annexationist threat that persisted long after Confederation helped to sustain it. On the other hand, twentieth century war generated integrationist trends. During the last sixty years or so the United States was transformed from hostile power to benevolent friend, and whole generations of Canadians grew up with the image of the United States as "our good neighbour to the south." This variety of after-dinner rhetoric often obscured the hard issues separating the two North American nations, but it certainly caught the essence of both official and popular opinion in the years after 1917.

What Canadians thought then and think now of the United States helps to shape their judgments of what the nature of the Canadian-American relationship was, is, and ought to be. The image of the good neighbour rested upon a benign view of United States policy at home and abroad. From this perspective, students of Canadian-American relations sought essentially to explain the dynamics of this

continental success story and, as in the Carnegie Endow-
ment's series *The Relations of Canada and the United
States,* largely tended to portray it as a model of peaceful
international relations that the rest of the world would do
well to follow.[1]

In the late 1950s and 1960s, a much more critical
perspective on American domestic and foreign policies
began to take form. The criticism of American social
commentators interacted with a developing nationalism
in Canada to create a somewhat different view of the
United States, one which altered the perspective of many
Canadians on the nature of the Dominion's relationship
with its neighbour. If America was best understood as an
imperial power, as some argued, then the dual relationship
had to be conceived of as an imperial relationship, not just
as good neighbourhood. And from this perspective the key
question was not how Canada and the United States had
become such good neighbours in the twentieth century;
rather it was how best to understand the process by which
Canada had negotiated her relationship with the imperial
power.[2]

In this more critical international milieu, it was not
surprising that Harold Innis' work would be rediscovered
and reassessed. Perhaps Canada's greatest economic historian and social thinker, Innis had anticipated the current
critique with his assertion that Canada had passed from
colony to nation to colony in less than a hundred years —
from a ward of the British Empire to a satellite of the new
American imperium. "We may dislike American influence,"
he wrote in 1948, "we may develop a Canadian under-
ground movement, but we are compelled to yield to American policy."[3] The fate of Canadian sovereignty under the
dominance of Pax Americana alarmed Innis, but he could
hold out little hope. "Canada has had no alternative but to
serve as an instrument of British imperialism and then of

American imperialism"[4]

Innis had noted the importance of American participation in the two world wars in explaining American
dominance, and this point, though underdeveloped in his
brilliant analyses, converged with some of the more perceptive of recent American critics. In *Roots of War,* for
example, Richard Barnet emphasized the extraordinary
growth of national security agencies occasioned by the
American mobilization in the Second World War. Arthur
Schlesinger, Jr., also delineated the 1941 war's impact on
the evolution of 'the imperial presidency.' Others have
noted the enormous expansion in America's global reach as
a result of that conflict. As the war ended in 1945, the
United States controlled 434 military bases around the
globe; before the war it had controlled Guam, Hawaii, and
the Philippines. Of these bases 195 were in the Pacific
which, with Japan's defeat, had become an American lake.
By 1944 the United States produced 45 percent of the
world's ammunition supply, and by the summer of 1945
America possessed a monopoly on the most destructive
weapon of all.[5]

The extension of American national power abroad was
accompanied by attempts at the systemic coordination of
military, economic and governmental institutions at home.
The creation of the Pentagon and the passage of the
National Security Act in 1947 both symbolized these
trends, and critics have labelled the institutional results
diversely as a new industrial state, a warfare state, and a
military-industrial complex. Whatever the name, the meaning is the same. All are indicative of the institutional
trappings of empire that Franz Schurmann has recently
summarized:

> Historically every empire has rested on a tripod of strength; an
> economy that spanned and in some way united its domains; a

monopoly of military power absolute within its domains and
adequate for security at its borders; and a political force that
emanated from its state, particularly the central executive.[6]

In the view of Schurmann and others, it was this kind of
institutional reality that characterized the United States in
the years immediately after 1945, the high point, in retrospect, of American imperial power.[7]

Accepting the view that the United States is indeed an
imperial power, what patterns can be discerned in Canada's
negotiation of her evolving relationship with the metro-
pole? The war years seem to us particularly important in
trying to answer this question. For one thing, wartime
mobilization accelerated America's thrust for empire, in
part a result of Britain's decline. For another, both world
wars stimulated in the United States a coordination of
major institutional orders on behalf of the nation's war-
making power that would become a constant feature of
American life as it entered the Cold War era. It is true, as
James Eayrs argued in a review of the first edition of this
book,[8] that peacetime relations are important too. Of
course they are, but in war American imperial power has
operated on a global scale with world-wide objectives.
Canadian-American relations in wartime, in other words,
though in the past have held the outlines of the future
within them.

On the other hand, one of those who reviewed *Canadian-
American Relations in Wartime,* Professor John English,
was certainly correct to observe that government officials
did not orchestrate all the major changes in the continental
relationship.[9] One of the key points revealed by recent
research is the central place of private decision-making on
both sides of the border. Evidence on this point can be
found in virtually every area of Canadian life — from the
influence on Western farm movements to the expansion of

American business techniques and forms. Additionally, the popular enthusiasm in Canada for varieties of American culture and technology must obviously be taken into account in any comprehensive analysis of Canadian-American relations.

But one need not go so far as some recent commentators, most notably some Canadian political scientists, to argue that such evidence renders notions of imperialism inapplicable as a perspective on Canadian-American relations.[10] Nor need one agree with the suggestion of John Holmes, the dean of Canadian commentators on foreign policy, that "the long history of Canada-United States struggle for control of the territory of North America had such a happy ending for the lesser power that it raises doubts about the innate American appetite for imperialism."[11] Nonetheless any conception of American imperialism must be complex enough to account for the voracious appetite of Canadian consumers for American goods and culture and broad enough to encompass the kind of unanticipated consequences of Canadian policies, such as that which turned a National Policy of protective tariffs intended as a foundation for Canadian industry into a lever for American branch plant expansion.[12]

It may indeed be useful to distinguish expansionism from imperialism, as Schurmann does in *The Logic of World Power*. In his view, the initiative for expansion occurs in society rather than in the state; from private, not public decision-making; and it is incremental, not consciously designed. To Schurmann "imperialism as a vision and a doctrine has a total, world wide quality."[13] With this formulation, we can consider that Canada has felt the impact of continuous American expansionism since 1867, but only since World War II has it had also to negotiate with American imperialism conceived as global power. It is the difference between the haphazard branchplant expansionism before 1939 and the self-conscious encouragement by American officals of the development of Canadian raw materials production in the 1950s.[14]

How then can we characterize Canada's negotiations with the American imperium in the twentieth century and particularly in wartime? There are, we believe, four important responses:

1. *The entrepeneurial response.* Stated baldly, Canada has tried to cash in on the extension of American national power. This has been an enduring theme of the Canadian interaction with American expansionism, but it has taken on added meaning with the Canadian effort to break into the imperial American defence market, particularly during and after the Second World War. In the process and in the traditional Canadian fashion, the Dominion government has played a selling and promoting function through Crown corporations. The object of such agencies as the Canadian War Mission of the Great War and War Supplies Limited in the Second World War has been to promote Canadian businesses in the United States. The Canadian Commercial Corporation carried out a similar task in the post-war period, and the succession of Defense Sharing agreements between the two countries indicates just how important such sales were to Ottawa.[15]

It is worth emphasizing the self-consciousness with which Canadian officials have tried to anticipate such developments. In the immediate postwar years, for example, when Canada faced a dollar shortage, Canadians lobbied in Ottawa to have the U.S. Government buy Canadian raw materials for the American strategic stockpile. And both before and after the Second World War, Canadians stressed the nearness and security of Canadian raw materials; indeed the development of this resource base is one of the major themes of Canadian economic history during the 1950s. C.D. Howe, the architect of Canada's mineral and industrial development, caught the spirit of the postwar era in a prescient speech in Parliament in December 1947: "As the mineral reserves of the United States are diminished, it [is] logical that attention will turn increasingly to Canadian mineral and associated hydro power resources."[16]

2. *The bureaucratic response.* Often competing with the entrepeneurial response, often complementary to it, has been the effort to rationalize these relationships, to embody them in regular administrative arrangements and procedural principles. The Hyde Park Declaration is an excellent illustration of the search for principles — as well as of the casual way of embodying them into practice. Similar arrangements took shape during the postwar years in Canada's seeking and finding ways to share in Marshall Plan largesse in 1948-9. Other examples are abundant, most notably in the military relations between the two countries. The route from the Permanent Joint Board on Defence through to NORAD is a straight line example of the rationalization of Canadian-American military-economic relationships.

3. *Quiet diplomacy.* In searching for special treatment in the United States, Canada has preferred to deal with the American imperium through its chief executive. There was a long war history behind the development of such attitudes. In the Great War, Canadian business bureaucrats had been scornful of the confusion and delay that characterized America's 1917 efforts. "This free loose Democracy," Sir Joseph Flavelle of the Imperial Munitions Board grumped, "is not well adapted for war or war decisions."[17] The problem was the diffusion of power, its sharing by too many politicians and bureaucrats and the struggle for it at all levels. Similar complaints abounded in the Second World War, and Lester Pearson found that "at times commitments to other governments made on one level in Washington were not or could not be fully implemented on another.

This was not due to bad faith," Pearson realized, "but to the lack of co-ordination of the activity and authority of so many unrelated decision-makers."[18] Canadian critics made the same observations in the Cold War years, too.[19]

The problem was that the Americans were not enough like us. They had no War Measures Act to concentrate all power in the Cabinet and they lacked the splendid virtues of the parliamentary system about which Canadians traditionally waxed superior. In such circumstances, the best Canadians could hope for was that the President would receive more authority, that the aggrandizement of executive powers would continue apace. It was not that Canadians were afraid to try their hand at interest group politics in Washington — the essays in this book provide ample proof that they were not. It was simply that if they lost at this game, they could then try a direct appeal to the President, as one nation to another. "If you could perhaps have a general word with the President on the subject," Norman Robertson wrote to Mackenzie King of one such small crisis in 1943, "this would, I am sure, do much more good than formal complaints through the diplomatic channels."[20] Exactly, and often such tactics worked.

In such a situation, "quiet diplomacy" was a useful tack to follow. It was far better to stay out of public battles in the newspapers, out of the glare of democratic scrutiny in the United States. It was better to manoeuver behind the scenes than to stir up the plethora of regional, political and state interests opposed to special deals. From the Canadian government's point of view, much more could be achieved in this way — and the results tend to bear this out from the IMB-Ordnance Department agreement, through Ogdensburg, Hyde Park and Defence Production Sharing arrangements.

4. *No questions asked.* Quiet diplomacy presupposed a willingness to keep silent, to ask no hard questions about

the purpose and nature of the American empire. And to the end of the 1950s few Canadians raised any such questions. Despite the rhetoric in Canada about the moralism of Canada's internationalism, Canadian officials and attentive publics have been extraordinarily pragmatic in negotiating with the empire. We have been as self-interested as the other nations who have accommodated themselves to the new order of things; unlike many other states, however, Canadians have been remarkably successful in working out their arrangements, in the short-term at least.

And yet, now that we are freed from many of the Cold War shibboleths and now that the dark side of the American empire has been laid bare by the Vietnamese agony, we should be able to see more clearly some of the trade-offs that were made. If quiet diplomacy was such a success why has there been such an extraordinary penetration of American influence and control in contemporary Canadian life, in the economy and in defence policy? Or was penetration the trade-off for the successful quiet diplomacy? These essays cannot provide the answers but we hope that they might raise some questions and stimulate some second thoughts. That, at any rate, was and is our intention.

NOTES

1. On the Carnegie series and its intent, see Carl Berger, *The Writing of Canadian History,* Toronto, 1976, ch. 6.

2. Irving L. Horowitz, "The Hemispheric Connection," *Queen's Quarterly,* Autumn, 1973, pp. 327 ff. and esp. 355.

3. Mary Quayle Innis, ed., *Essays in Canadian Economic History,* Toronto, 1956, p. 422; Berger, pp. 191 ff.

4. Innis, p. 405.

5. Richard J. Barnet, *Roots of War,* New York, 1972, esp. part I; Arthur Schlesinger, Jr., *The Imperial Presidency,* Boston, 1972, *passim;* Stephen E. Ambrose, *Rise to Globalism: American Foreign Policy 1938-70,* Baltimore, 1972, p. 68.

6. Franz Schurmann, *The Logic of World Power*, New York, 1974, p. xxiii.

7. The critical literature on the so-called military-industrial complex is enormous. Useful guides include T.A. Meeker, ed., *The Military-Industrial Complex*, Los Angeles, 1973; Carroll W. Pursell, Jr., ed., *The Military-Industrial Complex*, New York, 1972; Steven Rosen, ed., *Testing the Theory of the Military-Industrial Complex*, Lexington, 1973. See also Charles C. Moskos, Jr., "The Concept of the Military-Industrial Complex: Radical Critique or Liberal Bogey?", *Social Problems* 21, Spring, 1974, pp. 498 ff.

8. *Toronto Star*, March 1, 1975.

9. In *Canadian Forum*, Nov.-Dec., 1974, pp. 52-3.

10. For a summary statement of this view as well as a useful introduction to the recent literature on Canadian-American relations, see John H. Redekop, "A Reinterpretation of Canadian-American Relations," *Canadian Journal of Political Science* 9, June, 1976, pp. 227 ff. See also Andrew Axline, *et al.,* eds., *Continental Community?*, Toronto, 1974, *passim.*

11. John W. Holmes, *Canada: A Middle-Aged Power,* Toronto, 1976, p. 21. See also Holmes' review of this book in *Books in Canada,* May, 1975, pp. 26 ff.

12. See Michael Bliss, "Canadianizing American Business: The Roots of the Branch Plant," in Ian Lumsden, ed., *Close the 49th Parallel,* Toronto, 1970, pp. 27 ff.

13. Schurmann, p. 6.

14. Contrast this with Stephen Scheinberg, "Invitation to Empire: Tariffs and American Economic Expansion in Canada," in Glenn Porter and Robert Cuff, eds., *Enterprise and National Development,* Toronto, 1973, pp. 80 ff. On the theme of American concern with Canadian raw materials production in the 1950s see Percy W. Bidwell, *Raw Materials: A Study of American Policy,* New York, 1958, esp. pp. 349-52.

15. On Canadian arms sales, see Ernie Regehr, *Making a Killing,* Toronto, 1975, *passim;* on defence-sharing, see Jon B. McLin, *Canada's Changing Defense Policy, 1957-63,* Baltimore, 1967, ch. 7 and appx. 2, and John Warnock, *Partner to Behemoth,* Toronto, 1970, pp. 239-40.

16. House of Commons *Debates,* December 10, 1947, p. 135.

17. Queen's University, J.W. Flavelle Papers, Box 4, Flavelle to Sir John Willison, May 1, 1917.

18. Lester Pearson, *Mike: The Memoirs of the Rt. Hon. Lester B. Pearson,* Toronto, 1972, I, p.220.

19. Arnold Heeney, *The Things that are Caesar's,* Toronto, 1972, p. 108.

20. Public Archives of Canada, W.L.M. King Papers, Norman Robertson to King, August 14, 1943 (file 2411).

CHAPTER ONE

ORGANIZING FOR WAR:
CANADA AND THE UNITED STATES
DURING WORLD WAR I

Warfare has always placed a premium on organizational ability. From primitive tribal skirmishes to the great land battles of Napoleon, each type of war has involved some form of coordinate activity. "From the particular characteristics of war," writes Mao Tse-tung, there arise a particular set of organizations, a particular series of methods and a process of a particular kind. The organizations are the armed forces and everything that goes with them."[1] When wars came to involve great parts of a nation's population and resources, and as they increased in intensity, duration and cost, their organizational requirements became more extensive and complex. Wars in the twentieth century have required a total preparedness, which means, as Hans Speier puts it, "large scale planning with an inflated bureaucratic organization its inevitable concomitant."[2] The state has to weld a populace into an instrument of unified action, and mobilize its entire ideological and material resources to serve the fighting forces. In so doing it enlarges the organizational apparatus by which it exerts its authority. To study a modern war then is to study an organizational phenomenon *par excellence*. It is to study a nation's capacity to organize itself.

3

When he considers the problem of organization for war, the ·student of society in wartime confronts a number of problems. The first he must face is that of analyzing the nature of the state's bureaucratic apparatus — the kind of agencies the state creates, the relationship among them, their functions and administrative techniques, and so on. In addition, there is the problem of determining the kind of relationships these instruments of state control establish with the groups and organizations which compose society in general. He must view the actions of the state in the context of private groups and organizations which are also in the process of adjusting to the challenge of war.[8]

In a democratic society voluntary groups continue to function in wartime. Some are forcibly broken up and cast adrift by the state, but others are strengthened, and still others are created for the first time. Established groups use the symbols of patriotism and cooperation to increase their membership and to undermine their antagonists, while groups that were once apathetic suddenly come alive under the stimulus of conflict. Because war so often clears the path for innovation, organizational zealots seize on its necessities to win public support for their own private schemes. Aspiring professional organizations seek status by linking their expertise to national preparedness. Also of great importance for the organizational side of war is the fact that as the state assumes a greater role, group activity in society accelerates in self-defence. Interest groups affected by government policy feel compelled to organize more efficiently so that they may profit from it: their lobbying techniques are improved, their internal structures strengthened, and their technical expertise marshalled for government conferences.[4]

But if the demands of modern war mean that all countries achieve great organization, not all countries mobilize in the same way. Many factors ensure that national organizations are shaped by war in different ways. These include specific historical developments before the war, the hold of such values as individualism and localism, and the organizational ability that the state and society had already shown.

Clearly the impact of the war organization will be important for the society.[5] Equally, the way the war organization is established can have an impact on foreign relations, on trade, on economic ties with other allied powers or friendly neutrals. This is especially true of the Canadian-American relationship, for both countries had their own forms of organization, their different systems of government, their own bureaucracies with separate, often conflicting interests. Events and necessity forced the two nations to cooperate with each other, and in order to comprehend the way the two national states meshed, one must first understand the bureaucratic systems with which each began the Great War. This study of war as a problem of organization, this exploration of some aspects of industrial mobilization, attempts to do this.

In both countries national mobilization demanded highly efficient organizations manned by experts. In-flation, manpower, fuel, food and munitions problems all stimulated attempts at industrial planning and economic and social controls. Emergency agencies emerged to rationalize the economy, increase production, conserve scarce materials and generally coordinate the life of the nation.

This process proceeded only slowly in Canada after her entry into the war in August, 1914, with "individuals rather than the government leading in action on behalf of the community"[6] until well into 1917. According to J. A. Corry, the reasons for the private nature of early Canadian mobilization lay in the fragmented condition of large sectors of Canadian industry, which made economic centralization very difficult, the pervasive popular belief in the virtue of free enterprise, and the paucity of reliable government data on the economy. But as the demands of war grew, the government inevitably moved toward greater state intervention. The need to deal with food shortages brought into existence a Board of Grain Supervisors and a Food Controller in the summer of 1917, the latter organization expanding into a Food Board the following year. A Fuel Controller was also appointed in 1917 with extensive powers to involve municipalities in the regulation, distribution and price of coal. By 1918 the War Trade Board was created as an agency which for the first time possessed the power to bring a degree of centralized direction to the economy. The subsequent passage of an anti-loafing law and the establishment of the Canada Registration Board were symptomatic of the hardening lines of bureaucratic coordination.[7]

For its part, the United States did not create the instruments of national coordination before it entered the war in April, 1917, despite the opportunity it had to observe the course of Canadian and European mobilization. True, the Wilson Administration set up in the fall of 1916 a Council of National Defense and Advisory Commission which began to think about mobilization, and the Council did eventually spawn a great number of emergency agencies. But it accomplished little before April.[8] Canadian Prime Minister Robert Borden was pleased to recall that, "The Government of the United States in its various departments and activities made about all the mistakes that had been observable in the war preparedness of each of the allied nations, and probably added a few on its own account."[9] On the other hand, it should not be forgotten that if the American government was hamstrung in preparedness by its own policy of peace, private groups labored under no such handicap. American manufacturers, for example, gained a great deal of valuable experience before 1917 by supplying munitions to the Allies. Some firms sold fuses, cartridge cases and other materials to the Canadian Shell Committee and Imperial Munitions Board, supplies without which Canadian manufacturers might not have been able to fill some of their British munitions contracts.[10]

After it declared war, the United States organized quickly enough, and in a few months it had even overtaken Canada. In solving the food problem, the American government took action before Canadian officials, despite its late start. Wilson placed Herbert Hoover in charge of a projected Food Administration in May, 1917, a month before W. J. Hanna became Food Controller in Canada. After his appointment Hanna visited Washington to discuss the principles of efficient business organization with the Great Engineer.[11]

The Committee of Public Information, the War Industries Board, the Fuel Administration and the War Trade Board and the other agencies which appeared in the summer and fall deluged their constituencies with innumerable rules and regulations. Increasingly both Canadian and American societies became subjected to bureaucratic principles as men, regions, and industries were classified and arranged on scales of priority. Government agencies sought to fit people into new institutional arrangements and to standardize their attitudes, something which of course the French-speaking in Canada bitterly resisted. The sociologist Raymond Aron has written that "The supreme laws of the nation at war may be summed up in two words. . . . 'organization' and 'rationalization.' Rules which in times of peace are applied to only certain enterprises, or at most in certain phases of its productive machinery, are in time of war applied to the whole country."[12]

These expanding networks of emergency agencies seem to have retained more connection with the established federal departments in Canada than was the case in the United States, but in both instances they shared the habit of relying heavily on private businessmen for their personnel. And understandably so. The military services lacked sufficient experience of economic problems and concepts of industrial planning to undertake mobilization unaided; civil service personnel were too small in numbers and too enmeshed in routine to respond adequately to the crisis. On the other hand, businessmen possessed the skills in handling personnel, supervising technical operations and managing administration which were now vital to an enlarged state bureaucracy. Moreover, they were skilled in the art of bargaining, and the state now had to have by its side men who were sensitive to the ceremony and ritual of the business game and who could therefore persuade the holders of private economic power to support its policies.[13]

Opening the councils of government to an influx of businessmen and making society so dependent on their skills in production was not without its dangers to the state. Woodrow Wilson, for one, apparently regarded the implications with such uneasiness that in 1916 he confided to his Secretary of the Navy, Josephus Daniels: " . . . if we enter this war, the great interests which control steel, oil, shipping, munitions factories, mines, will of necessity become dominant factors, and when the war is over our government will be in their hands. We have been trying, and succeeding to a large extent, to unhorse government by privilege. If we go into this great war all we have gained will be lost and neither you nor I will live long enough to see our country wrested from the control of monopoly."[14] And yet despite such evidence of suspicion toward big business on the eve of war, Wilson made every effort both before and after April, 1917, to gain support from America's corporate leaders.[15] Moreover, the zeal with which he pursued this goal suggests that in the last analysis he never really found friendly cooperation with the "great interests" incompatible with his programs for either war or peace. In 1917 he wrote to one southern senator who objected to the close cooperation established between business and government in Washington: "If anything in the law should make it necessary to dispense with [the services of businessmen], the government would be seriously and perhaps fatally embarrassed, inasmuch as we must in the circumstances have the cooperation of the men who are in actual control of the great business enterprises of the country."[16]

Besides playing an extensive part in government administration itself, businessmen and business groups stood in the vanguard of the movement for rationalization of the mobilization process. Private business leaders recognized that only a strong national power could stabilize the economy sufficiently to let them design the defences that would get them through the chaos of war. The fact that the state administration was partially staffed by business specialists made the idea of enlisting its support all the more acceptable. On January 8, 1918, in an act symbolic of the attitude of business in seeking government intervention, at least in the latter part of the war, a large delegation of Canadian manufacturers descended upon Ottawa to speak on behalf of plans for a War Trade Board then under consideration. According to the editor of the *Canadian Annual Review*, "they urged something similar to the U.S. War Industries Board as necessary in view of the great difficulties encountered by Canadian manufacturers in securing raw material from the United States since the entry of that country into the war."[17] On February 8 the Government did establish the Board under the chairmanship of Sir George Foster, the Minister of Trade and Commerce. The Board was to supervise export and import licenses, prevent waste in labor and raw materials, direct priority in the distribution of fuel, electricity, raw materials and partially finished products, consider the problem of essential and less essential industries, and encourage economic cooperation between Canada and the United States. Such functions held out the promise of more order and coherence in the mobilization of Canadian resources.[18]

Since the state had to deal with a great diversity of issues and to intervene in numerous areas of national life besides the economy, the new adminstrators included many people besides businessmen. Washington became a magnet for a wide diversity of people, all desirous of a place in the new war machinery so they could pull the levers of power and assist the war effort at the same time. The war caused great excitement among innovators of all kinds — liberal intellectuals, scientific management enthusiasts, social scientists and others. In a nation mobilizing for action, each saw the possibility of achieving his long sought programs for social progress. Social worker Edward T. Devine caught their mood when he wrote in the summer of 1917 that

> A luxuriant crop of new agencies is springing up. We scurry back and forth to the national capital; we stock offices with typewriters and new letterheads; we telephone feverishly, regardless of expense, and resort to all the devices of efficient "publicity work" ... It is all very exhilarating, stimulating, intoxicating.[19]

And reformers found much to be enthusiastic about in the war. As Allen Davis has recently shown, the war was the culmination of many progressive reforms — in labor practices, in social insurance, public housing, health insurance and more. So successful was the progressive crusade to eliminate the evils of prostitution that the Commission on Training Camp Activities which worked with the Army closed down every red light district in the country, and thus permitted America to field what one man called, "the cleanest army since Cromwell's day."[20] Emphasis on a strong and healthy fighting force encouraged the extension of state power on behalf of social reform. Regulations were introduced requiring vaccination against smallpox and inoculation against typhoid and cholera in the Canadian Expeditionary Forces, an action which typifies the way in which the military services in both countries became channels through which the state tried to shape the habits and values of its citizens.[21]

As stated at the outset, a nation takes on the character of an administrative state during wartime, a state managed by commissions of experts or specialists. So it is critically important for us to understand how these various emergency bodies exercise their mandates. Their actions are aimed at mobilizing the nation for war, but how they do this — indeed whether they do this — depends on many factors, including the kind of support they receive from their clientele, the relationships they establish among each other and with regular departments, and the assumptions and values of the people who staff them. So many descriptions of the home front during World War I in Canada and the United States survey the moves toward centralization, but neglect to explore the effects of these kinds of factors. To illustrate some of their implications, let us look briefly by way of case study at the evolution and operation of the United States War Industries Board, a major agency in the American program of industrial mobilization.[22]

This agency was established as a subordinate part of the Council of National Defense at the end of July, 1917, the outgrowth of a number of earlier, less satisfactory arrangements. Joining Frank A. Scott, a Cleveland manufacturer, and chairman of the Board, were Bernard M. Baruch, a Wall Street speculator and early preparedness advocate, as commissioner of raw materials, Robert S. Lovett, chairman of the Union Pacific Railroad, as commissioner of priorities, Robert S. Brookings, retired millionaire and president of Washington University of St. Louis, as commissioner of finished products, Hush Frayne, an AFL organizer, as commissioner of labor, and also Col. Palmer E. Pierce, from the Army, and Rear Admiral F. F. Fletcher from the Navy. The WIB's duties were defined as follows.[23]

> The Board will act as a clearing house for the war industry needs of the Government, determine the most effective ways of meeting them and the best means and methods of increasing production, including the creation or extension of industries demanded by the emergency, the sequence and relative urgency of the needs of the different Government services, and consider price factors, and in the first instance the industrial and labor aspects of the problems involved and the general questions affecting the purchase of commodities.

Despite the hopes that this agency raised, instability in its structure plagued it from the very beginning. The presence of the two military representatives indicates that the functions of the Board rested on the promise of cooperation from the services. The Board operated in a kind of twilight zone between private and public institutions, greatly dependent on good will from both sides. Its effectiveness also depended on the degree of harmony it achieved among its various units. Without synchronization in its internal operations it could hardly expect to act as an agency for national economic coordination. Furthermore, unlike such agencies as the Food and Fuel Administration, the Board was not established by Congressional statute, and so was without firm legal foundation. Its members were extremely sensitive about pushing their constituency too hard. As much from necessity as from conviction, the WIB administrators chose voluntary cooperation over arbitrary fiat. This policy of opportunism compounded its early instability.

When the Board did not receive the full cooperation of the military services in subsequent months it floundered badly, gradually losing its credibility among businessmen. Military officials were not yet convinced that they had to accept central economic coordination, or to share their mandates for mobilization. The Secretaries of War and the Navy, jealous of their departmental preserves, assisted them in their independent course. As autumn gave way to winter, fuel shortages threatened, even as supplies sat unused at railroad terminals. Rumours spread about possible curtailment of less essential industries. Increasingly disillusioned, Baruch, Lovett and the Administration's other business advisors vented their anger during the congressional inquest into the war effort in January and strongly favored the drive for centralization sponsored by the United States Chamber of Commerce. "Executive authority simply cannot be efficiently exercised by boards and committees," Lovett explained to Colonel House. "The stronger and abler the members, the more inefficient the board will be, for each member will have ideas of his own, and will maintain them. Protracted debate will follow. I believe strongly in a single executive for any task when large."[24] Businessmen familiar with the economics of the war wanted a chance to grasp full, concentrated power to bring some real discipline to the mobilization. Authority had to be centralized. "It must be done," warned one business administrator, "or we will wreck our industries."[28] It is ironic that Canadian manufacturers should be campaigning in January, 1918, for a War Trade Board modelled along the lines of an agency which in the eyes of many American businessmen had by that time been thoroughly discredited.

Under pressure from all sides to create a ministry of munitions, President Wilson moved to appease his critics, and made the WIB the center of his attention. He finally severed the WIB's ties with the Council of National Defense and gave it an independent life. He defined its functions more clearly, elevated Baruch to the chairmanship, and concentrated final authority in Baruch's hands for all questions except price fixing. This subject fell to a separate Price Fixing Committee under Robert Brookings, with Baruch an ex officio member. The appointment of a single chairman in place of the Board's former executive committee represented a move toward greater centralization. Yet at the same time, the President left all purchasing functions — the actual expenditure of funds — with the military departments. In other words he baulked at business demands for complete centralization of all purchasing powers in a single civilian agency to be run by some kind of munitions czar.

In subsequent months, top WIB officials still bemoaned their lack of legislative authority, but after the spring of 1918 their work moved more smoothly. Now that the Board's star had risen in the bureaucratic firmament of wartime Washington, more and more business groups discovered the advantages of cooperating with it; and the WIB increased its commodity sections to care for their individual needs and improve their relationship to the overall supply program. By this time too the Army, which had to reorganize its own operations during the winter, moved swiftly and in the summer of 1918 it sent representatives to the Board's commodity sections, and participated more willingly in the kind of economic coordination the Board sought to offer. Furthermore, the process of bureaucratization taking place in the Board's internal operations brought its own stability. Though the sources of insecurity in the WIB's environment had not wholly disappeared by the fall of 1918, these various improvements meant it could now function with a far greater sense of both security and power.

Several aspects about the way the Board functioned during its evolution are worth noting. First of all, the Board depended much more on bargaining and negotiation with business groups than upon a series of fixed rules enforced by governmental police action. Its very instability as an organization during much of its life made it difficult to apply continuous pressure or to hold out against hostile interest. In the difficult days of the winter of 1917-1918, for example, the Board informed the President that unless the government was willing to take over and run an industry as a last resort, there was no point in price fixing because there was "no law providing penalties or other means for enforcing obedience to the order."[26] Because no such legislation remedying this situation was ever forthcoming, set limits were placed on what the WIB could do by way of regulating price. Even after the Board recovered its health and the President established a formal Price Fixing Committee, the Committee preferred to negotiate an agreement with the dominant producers in an industry and leave them to bring the rest of the trade into line, and to take whatever police measures they felt necessary.[27] Lewis Haney, who worked as an economist with the Federal Trade Commission during the war observed:

> The work of the Price-Fixing Committee of the War Industries Board was in the main a "trading proposition." While considerable pressure could be, and in some cases was, brought to bear upon an industry, there was generally an effort to reach an agreement, in which considerable bargaining was used. The Price-Fixing Committee knew that the government must depend upon the cooperation of the industry in order to prevent evasion and to secure the service which was so important.[28]

This comment is relevant to all areas of the Board's operations. The Board could only be certain of compliance if industry agreed with its regulations; beyond that the success was uncertain. The Board's ability to fulfill its mandate to fix prices, curtail less essential production, or to conserve raw material was by no means a foregone conclusion despite the myth which grew up about its dictatorial powers. Furthermore, we can conclude that under these circumstances industrial planning was based less on a coherent philosophy or economic blueprint, than on a simple coordination of semi-private agreements sanctioned by public authority.

The second point worth emphasizing is that the WIB obviously *shared* power with the very groups it sought to regulate. Board decisions were heavily influenced by the representatives of private groups, even to the choice of personnel to staff the Board's commodity sections. Bernard Baruch spoke to this point when he told the representatives of the cotton fabrics industry: "You are just as much of the Government as we are; we could not get along without you, whatever we may think is wise and proper. I feel we have got to have your assistance — we cannot get along without you; we have not the power or the knowledge."[29] Arch Shaw, a Chicago magazine publisher and business theorist, made this approach the guiding philosophy of the WIB's Conservation Division. He explained after the war that:

> The function of the Commercial Economy Board [the name of Shaw's committee before March, 1918] was to conserve our resources and our facilities. No board and no individual was qualified to perform that function in all the diverse industries and trades of the United States. So the Commercial Economy Board simply called in these various industries and told them the Government's needs and enlisted them as Government officials so far as their industries were concerned.[30]

That power was shared meant that private business groups had an opportunity to use public power to protect themselves. They could hide under the wing of the WIB and shield themselves from the economic storms of war. Price agreements could place floors under markets where the demand was weak and ceilings where the demand was dangerously high; priority regulations could feed the starving as well as regulate the greedy, and cooperation with a public agency encouraged the kind of industry-wide agreements which if undertaken privately were susceptible to legal prosecution. As Robert Brookings of the Price Fixing Committee explained to one trade group: "We meet together as one organization, one group, one industry. The Government becomes your partner in trying to do something that you couldn't do alone very well, in assisting you to stabilize the market."[31]

WIB administrators believed that their task in industrial mobilization included saving and strengthening the country's industrial structure for the postwar years. As Baruch wrote to Daniel Guggenheim in June, 1918, "Just as much as it is my duty to see that there is no profiteering is it my duty to see that no vital industry, especially one like the smelting and refining business, shall be injured or destroyed."[32] With their emphasis on economic stability, rationality, efficiency and industry-wide cooperation, these men sought to extend through state organization the values associated with modern corporate capitalism.[33] During the war they experimented with national institutional arrangements which would enhance its advance, institutional arrangements which Presidents Hoover and Roosevelt would enlarge upon twenty years later in their efforts to save capitalism itself.

The war served an important function in educating the new public administrators to the relationships which could be established among different kinds of private organizations and then combined in turn with public power. In Canada a good example of this trend is evident in the agitation among business and academic organizations which culminated in the formation of the National Research Council.[34] A similar development in the United States is to be found in the way in which, during the evolution of the WIB, businessmen strove to draw the military services into closer harmony with business organizations and values. Ironical as it may sound, business administrators wanted to stamp out what they regarded to be an excessive individualism in the armed services. In their inter-service and inter-bureau rivalries for military supplies the Army and Navy demonstrated a competitive behaviour which corporate businessmen like Robert Brookings had long since renounced. Brookings and his colleagues had already accepted the usefulness of long-range cooperative planning in disciplining and stabilizing economic markets. In general terms what took place during the war in both Canada and the United States was a battle by the "cooperators" in private and public institutions against the individualists and traditionalists who had not yet seen the value of institutional cooperation guided by overarching national agencies.

The men in the higher echelons of the WIB caught a vision of institutional coordination for economic production and stability which never left them. And the same was true of some of the military officers who proved sympathetic to the WIB's goals. The ease with which the new administrators moved among business, military and government institutions in the postwar years is indicative of this shared vision. There are a number of interesting and fairly well known examples of this phenomenon. Army General Hugh Johnson, a friend of the WIB in the service, joined George Peek, the WIB's Commissioner of Finished Products in the agricultural implement business after the war, joined Bernard Baruch's entourage when the enterprise failed, and ultimately entered the New Deal as head of the National Recovery Administration. George Peek had been deeply impressed during the war with the need for business-government cooperation for economic health, and he retained this perspective on economic problems into the postwar period. He never did leave public life. He took up the farm problem in the twenties and headed the Agricultural Adjustment Administration in the New Deal. Walter Gifford, a statistician with American Telephone and Telegraph before the war and company president after 1925, served as Director of the Council of National Defense in the war, and was brought back into government service in 1931 by Herbert Hoover as chairman of the President's Emergency Committee for Employment. Alexander Legge of the International Harvester Company who supervised Allied purchasing for the WIB, also found his way into the Hoover Administration as chairman of the Federal Farm Board. Johnson, Peek, Gifford and Legge, like Hoover himself, remained enamoured of the idea of achieving a stable productive economy not through extensive state controls, but through voluntary cooperation among private organizations under the benevolent eye of a friendly national agency like the wartime WIB.[35]

Voluntary cooperation could be extended across international borders, too. Indeed it was far better to strike arrangements on a cooperative basis than to be forced into them; one very good example of this was the way in which the Imperial Munitions Board moved to fill the shortfall in British munitions orders by turning to the American market, a transaction of special benefit to Canada's war industry.

CHAPTER TWO

SYMBOL OF A RELATIONSHIP:
THE ORDNANCE DEPARTMENT-
IMB AGREEMENT OF 1917

After weeks of negotiations, the Imperial Munitions
Board of Canada reached an arrangement with the Ordnance Department of the United States Department of War
in November, 1917 designed to bring American munitions
orders to Canada. In the words of its chairman, Sir Joseph
Flavelle, the IMB would

> make all arrangements in connection with the contracts, and
> subsequently see to their completion. We will make all
> disbursements on behalf of the United States Government, and
> generally, act for them in practically the same manner as we
> are acting for the Imperial Government, except that in the one
> case we are part of the [British] Ministry of Munitions, while
> in the other we are only Agents for the Ordnance Department
> of the United States Government.[1]

When he informed the Prime Minister, Sir Robert Borden,
of this new development, Flavelle noted that at the
moment it covered only a single transaction. He hoped,
however, "that other business will follow which we may be
able to apportion to Canadian manufacturers without
interfering with the products which we are instructed to
secure for the Imperial authorities."[2] He was not disap-
pointed. The developing relationship was formalized the

following month and extended "to cover and include the procurement of ordnance material of all classes."[3]

It was a remarkable arrangement in many ways. It turned the Canadian arm of the British Munitions Ministry into an agent of the U.S. government as well, and it transformed its chief employee, the IMB chairman, into a virtual mediator in munitions production between the British and American governments. It added a continental function to an Imperial organization, and all for the domestic purpose of maintaining economic prosperity in Canada. For Sir Joseph Flavelle and Sir Robert Borden no more intended to sell out Canadian industry by the Ordnance Department — IMB Agreement of 1917 than did C. D. Howe and Mackenzie King with the Hyde Park Declaration of 1941. On the contrary, they intended to employ American means to serve Canadian ends.

The agreement simply crystallized the economics of Anglo-Canadian-American relations. It institutionalized the continental nature of Canada's munitions production, which had been dependent from the beginning upon American supplies of coal, steel and machine tools. The agreement promised to bring a segment of that process full circle, since the U.S. government intended to supply raw materials and component parts for its Canadian contracts. Combining imperial and continental functions through the IMB, the agreement also underscored the way in which Canada's wartime prosperity had become linked to the United States as well as to Great Britain. It symbolized the North American dimension of the war-induced prosperity which both Canada and the United States shared at the expense of the Allies in general and of Great Britain in particular. The demands of the Great War, no less than of World War II and the Cold War, encouraged a continental approach to the North American economy.

In the broadest perspective, the IMB-Ordnance agreement was one of a series of consequences for Canada of the radical alteration which occurred in the structure of international finance during the Great War. It signified, albeit indirectly, that great transformation in the economic relationship between Britain and the United States, and in Canada's relations with both. Its emergence is best understood against the broad and shifting contours of Atlantic finance.

British and Allied commitments in the U.S. had grown rapidly during the years of American neutrality. American exports increased at a stunning rate. Britain's expenditures totalled $469 million from August to December, 1916, for example, and $427 million from December, 1916, to April, 1917. During the three years ending 30 June, 1917, the firm of J. P. Morgan alone, acting as an agent for the government of Britain and France, shipped to the Allies goods valued at $31.1 billion, or about twenty-nine percent of total American exports. In return for these mounting imports the Allies provided more than $1 billion in gold, sold for dollars $1.4 billion of their American securities, and borrowed about $2.4 billion in U.S. financial markets to April, 1917. While Britain's adverse trade balance with the U.S. stood at £72.9 million in 1911-1913, it jumped to £181.3 million in 1915, to £227.3 million in 1916, and to £316.3 million in 1917. The liquidation of American securities, begun in July, 1915, mounted inexorably finally to equal about seventy percent of British holdings by the end of 1919.[4]

The crux of the problem for Britain and the Allies was the shortage of dollar exchange, for as a student of British war finance notes, "upon the maintenance of an adequate supply of dollars at a reasonable price, depended the whole vast purchasing programme of food, materials and munitions for ourselves and our allies."[5] An exchange crisis in the summer of 1915 produced a private Anglo-French loan, for example, which even at $500 million was less than the British had needed.[6] Three issues of collateral notes were made between September, 1916, and January, 1917, and overdrafts with Morgan and Co., begun in May, 1916, totalled $395.5 million a year later.[7]

Throughout these years there was a continuous and significant interaction between the economics of Anglo-American relations on the one hand and the nature of Anglo-Canadian relations on the other. The gradual transformation of the first set of relations necessarily left an indelible mark on the second. At a minimum, Britain had to balance her commitments to Canada and the other Dominions so as to meet her exchange demands in the United States. In the heady optimism of August 1914, Britain might agree to finance the costs of the war for Canada, but within a few months that was clearly seen to be beyond Britain's financial resources. By the end of the year, Sir Thomas White, the Minister of Finance, was wiring London that he had been offered a loan in New York "but on sentimental grounds and on account pride London has had in furnishing Dominion money think American market should be left to our Provinces and municipalities."[8] Britain would continue to lend Canada money to pay for her expenses overseas, but sentiment was soon insufficient to secure financing for domestic expenditures in the metropolitan center. Increasingly Ottawa would have to find other sources of war finance.

A British refrain sounded consistently throughout the early years was that Canada could and should do more. Pressure on Ottawa increased as British exchange difficulties deepened in New York. In the summer of 1915, for example, London urged the Dominion to mobilize Canadian financial resources with a domestic loan backed by imperial guarantees, and it approved a Canadian proposal to have Ottawa float an American loan, the first in Canadian history.[9] This latter step was an action of no little historic significance, but it was justified easily enough by its contribution to Britain's exchange situation. While British officials negotiated for the Anglo-French loan of 1915, Canada's High Commissioner in London warned the Minister of Finance, Sir Thomas White, that the "Treasury suggests unofficially that Canada's production and exports are increasing so much that before long Canada may be able to provide her own money even for war expenses."[10] Although this did not occur, in the summer of 1916 the British did ask Ottawa to cover the Canadian costs of the IMB's operations.

Sir Thomas White and his colleagues in the Borden government could hardly be unaware of imperial financial exigencies and they would augment Canada's contributions as the war dragged on. They could not be expected to sympathize with every British request, however, or with the coercive economic power and slightly patronizing attitude these requests so thinly veiled. White told Flavelle in August, 1916 that "I have no doubt the Imperial Chancellor is heavily burdened; he may consider that I am not heavily burdened. I cannot allow his judgment to prevail; I will only be governed by my own judgment."[11] The Minister of Finance's judgment was almost invariably cautious. He turned down the British suggestion of a domestic loan for war expenditures in 1915, and he refused to increase his credits to the IMB in the following year. White "has advised repeatedly Imperial Munitions Board that in view of his rapidly increasing war expenditures he could not undertake to make further advances," the Governor General telegraphed to the Colonial Secretary on August 5, 1916.[12] White told Flavelle the same thing in late 1916: "it would be a serious mistake to make any definite engagement. We can only take up the situation from time to time in Canada and arrange such credits as may be possible having regard to the condition of the banks and our finances."[13] Any Canadian aid to the IMB, White obviously believed, had to be at the convenience of the Canadian government and not on a predetermined, obligatory basis. In practice the consequences were much the same, but the principle was an important one for the Finance Minister.

Aside from White's understandable desire to retain the utmost flexibility and autonomy for his own policies, his frequent resentment of inexorable British demands seemed legitimate enough on other grounds. From his perspective it seemed that the British failed constantly to understand the extent either of his own financial problems at home or of the growing scale of Canadian aid to Britain. In addition, as a cautious banker before he entered the government in 1911, White initially took a very limited view of war finance, though in this opinion he merely reflected the conventional wisdom in Canadian ruling circles. He was determined, for instance, to have Canadian banks first serve his own financial program before they advanced loans to Britain. He was reluctant to raise funds through taxation, and he was skeptical at first about the promises held out by domestic war loans. Events ultimately forced him to yield on these points. The banks did offer direct loans to the British government;[14] a business profits tax emerged in 1916; a federal income tax followed in 1917; and domestic war loans mounted as the years passed. Ultimately, to White's surprise and that of Canada's bankers, the Dominion would draw the bulk of her war finances from internal borrowing. In retrospect, the tremendous increase in the Canadian financial contribution to the war effort might seem inevitable, but it did not appear so to men at the time. In the postwar years, of course, Sir Thomas for one would not fail to make a case for his foresight.[15]

Sir Joseph Flavelle certainly had no illusions about the financial policies of Sir Thomas White and the Borden government, though he would defend them against unreasonable criticism from British officials. His problems was that he had to work with both White and the Treasury in London, and sometimes the IMB chairman found himself caught in the middle. With White he could agree that obligatory advances to the Board were unwise; with the British he could bemoan the Finance Minister's tight-fistedness. But as the chief spokesman for and protector of a burgeoning munitions industry, Flavelle did everything within his power to keep his industrial plant at full production. Undue caution by either White and Canadian chartered bankers on the one hand or the British Treasury on the other was dangerous to his plans. The major danger, of course, lay with an increasingly desperate and hence parsimonious Treasury. But Flavelle was even more scornful of Canadian bankers, "this body of timid, fearful men."[16] The IMB Chairman's role as mediator between England and Canada was a difficult one, but unless Flavelle could prod both sides into settlements favourable to his agency the results could be disastrous to Canadian munitions production. The IMB-Ordnance Department Agreement, from this perspective, was one tactic in Flavelle's broader strategy of full production.

U.S. entry into the war in April, 1917, raised a host of questions about the future of war finance in both London and Ottawa. Washington now replaced New York as the center of American finance and public officials joined private bankers at the locus of power. "As England was the sole financial resource of the Allies in the war against Napoleon," commented Sir Cecil Spring-Rice, the British Ambassador, "so the United States are our sole resource from the financial point of view at the present moment."[17] On the day after the declaration of war, U.S. Treasury

Secretary William Gibbs McAdoo approached Congress with a plan to raise $7 billion, with $3 billion earmarked for · Allied loans.[18] This remarkable shift in economic power from Britain to the United States was not easily accomplished. One British representative touched on the psychic dimension of the change after a few days on the scene in Washington. Exasperated with the unrealistic attitudes of his colleagues back in London, Lord North-cliffe wrote that "Members of the Cabinet should understand that our attitude towards the United States Government is that of beggars."[19]

There were other problems. Treasury Secretary McAdoo, now the key official in Anglo-American finance, jealously guarded his prerogatives and strove eagerly to augment his power both within the Wilson administration and with the Allies. He, in turn, had also to consider Congressional strictures on the extension of Allied loans, as well as the suspicion among American business interests over Britain's postwar economic goals.[20]

In the subsequent weeks of May and June all these frictions and more converged in a single issue: the payment of those private Allied debts incurred during the period of neutrality. At issue with the British was who should take responsibility for an overdraft with the J. P. Morgan Company, Washington or London. The Wilson Administration's distrust of the Morgan's complicated the problem, as did McAdoo's desire to make all future loans conditional upon the coordination of both Allied financial demands and their subsequent U.S. purchasing. In June the American Treasury peremptorily cut off all loans. Whitehall was engulfed in panic. The Foreign Secretary, Lord Balfour, cabled President Wilson's chief adviser, Colonel House, on June 29 that "We seem on the verge of a financial disaster which would be worse than a defeat in the field."[21] British representatives, aided by Colonel

House, lobbied strenuously to contain the issue, and the apparent willingness of the British both to shoulder the overdraft and to support McAdoo's ideas on central coordination brought a degree of success. But even then, the crisis, though diffused, awaited the arrival of the curiously titled "High Commissioner for financial matters," Lord Reading, in September, 1917 for its final denouement.[22]

It was against this background of friction with the Americans as well as of such continuing problems as limited gold and diminishing dollar reserves that London determined in late spring to cut back its operations in Canada. The Canadian government was advised that the Chancellor of the Exchequer "does not see any way of meeting Imperial Munitions Department's purchases except through Canadian sources ... steps should be taken without delay to reduce that expenditure in Canada."[23] The cuts extended beyond munitions to such additional commodities as cheese and grains, and throughout the summer Canadian and British officials engaged in tense negotiations. Given the extraordinary leverage the British government had on the Canadian economy, the Borden government had ultimately to yield to the inevitable and shoulder more of the financial burdens of Canadian purchasing. They did not reach this position, however, without some strenuous, if futile bargaining.

The Treasury outlined several approaches Canada might take toward adjusting to British policy on June 30. These included further bank loans and the issuance of additional currency notes: "a stage of the war has now been reached," the Colonial Secretary informed Ottawa, "when, however regrettably, some risks must be taken. It is for the Canadian Government to weigh disadvantages of the course of action which we now urge upon them with the effect on the British Army's supply of munitions and the loss and confusion in which Canadian manufacturers would be involved if the Imperial Munitions Board were not in a position to meet their liabilities."[24] Sir Thomas White had already baulked at the idea of further bank loans and additional currency, and he seemed ready to do so again. It took an even more forceful telegram from Lloyd George himself to Borden to break White's resistance. The "only alternatives," the British Prime Minister said, "are that we should largely diminish orders placed in Canada or that Canada should make itself mainly responsible for financing those orders. We should be most reluctant to adopt the former course."[25] The British held all the best cards in this particular game, for Canadian prosperity, as London and Ottawa knew well, rested heavily on British war orders. In the end, the Canadian government acceded to most of the particular items at issue. It agreed, among other things, to increase its note circulation, to assist the IMB to the extent of $25 million a month from July to next December, to finance cheese purchases, and to contribute to the purchase of Canadian hay, oats and flour.[26]

There was one point, however, to which the Canadians held firm throughout these foredoomed negotiations. They insisted that they would commit themselves to a regular obligation to the IMB only "upon condition that the Treasury will without fail provide Imperial Munitions Board with fifteen million dollars from American sources during each of the said months."[27] White's original request had been for between $25 million and $50 million each month, but he would go no lower. His conditions became the *quid pro quo* of Canada's agreeing to a far greater financial contribution towards IMB purchases.

At issue here was Canada's own trade and exchange problem with the United States. According to Ottawa's figures, the Canadian deficit stood at $218,617,029 in

1914; $110,289,650 in 1915; $153,827,312 in 1916; and estimates were that it would reach $373,641,080 in 1917.[28] As Borden informed Lloyd George in July, "The balance of trade between Canada and United States is greatly in favour of the latter and New York exchange is now at a heavy premium here."[29] It was the same concern, no doubt, which prompted Borden to draw to London's attention the impact of American belligerency on Canada's relationship to U.S. money markets. "The position of our securities on the market is quite critical," he told the Prime Minister, "owing to Canadian securities being debarred from the American market since the entry of United States into the war."[30] Canadians, therefore, linked a settlement of Anglo-Canadian financial difficulties to the U.S. response to two requests: first, Ottawa's appeal for an exemption from the ban on foreign borrowing; and second, London's demand, at Canadian insistence, that $15 million each month of American loans to Britain be set aside for expenditure in Canada.

In the meantime Flavelle, like White and Borden, had to respond to the crisis engendered by the British threats. For one thing, the business community was unnerved about its future prospects, a dangerous state of affairs for the government, with a very difficult general election looming in the near future. The *Financial Post* reported the drying up of orders in August and forecast shutdowns and layoffs in the near future. "Canada," it predicted gloomily in September, "is entering a period of sharp readjustment. How the country will weather the storm remains to be seen."[31] Flavelle himself wrote to a British official that "I believe . . . a factor in our present situation is that we will strengthen the hands of stable Government by introducing as little business disturbance as possible by reason of unnecessarily shutting down munition plants."[32]

There were, in addition, growing instances of Canadian

manufacturers seizing their profits and selling off their munitions machinery to U.S. interests.[33] This only compounded Flavelle's problems, for any wholesale removal would turn what might conceivably be a temporary crisis into a permanent one. Naturally enough, Flavelle pleaded with Munitions Ministry officials to continue sufficient numbers of orders to maintain his Canadian plant capacity. He argued that the British authorities were not only losing an investment to the United States which they had largely underwritten with public funds, but they were also running the risk of having insufficient machining capacity to answer British calls in the future. Nevertheless, according to Flavelle, transfers across the border continued apace throughout the summer and fall. As a businessman himself, the Chairman, of course, could not very well expect Canadian businessmen to avert their eyes from lucrative opportunities to sell their machinery, but he worried about the trend. As the Munitions Ministry's agent in Canada this anxiety came naturally enough. In Flavelle's case, however, sentiment for the imperial tie and a genuine concern about Canadian industrial dependency on the United States supplemented his official concern. In the end, he felt obliged to press Borden to block U.S.-bound munitions machinery by order in council, arguing all the while that imperial self-interest required the maintenance of Canadian munitions capacity.[34]

Ultimately, only new orders would halt the drain of machinery to the United States. If Britain would not place them, perhaps the United States would. In 1916 Flavelle had been willing to have Canadian firms solicit American business on their own rather than to have their machines standing idle, but in the summer of 1917 he personally began actively and officially to seek ways and means to secure American orders. He inquired of his contacts in the British War Mission in Washington about various methods of approach to U.S. authorities, and he also sent his own emissaries south of the border in search of some way out of his dilemma.[35]

The crisis of 1917 clarified dramatically the ongoing interrelationships among Anglo-American-Canadian economic relations, particularly in the areas of finance and munitions production. Originating in large part along the Anglo-American axis, the crisis generated a pressure which doubled back on Anglo-Canadian relations to force a Canadian response. One significant component of this response was a far more serious mobilization of domestic financial resources and the first Victory Loan in the autumn of 1917. In addition, Finance Minister White began to search for a way to tap American funds and American markets. This tactic, it was hoped, would reduce Canada's adverse trade balance and also help retain manufacturing facilities. Financial and industrial problems were intertwined.

On the whole Ottawa was remarkably successful in achieving its economic goals vis-à-vis the United States at this point. Sir Thomas White took the financial issue in hand in late June. Determined to avoid direct borrowing from the United States government, White sought Treasury Secretary McAdoo's permission to float a short-term private loan. White made two central points in his presentation. First, American dollars would ensure a continuation of Canadian purchases in the United States. Second, with its great economic resources, America could easily afford this minor exemption. "I might point out to you that the balance of trade between Canada and [the] United States is greatly in your favour and this is a strong reason why we should be permitted to borrow," wrote White. "Unless we can obtain credit in [the] United States it would appear to me that our purchases there must necessarily fall off."[36] For his part, McAdoo inclined towards having the federal government provide a loan, though he did not press the point in this instance. Thomas Lamont of Morgan's, when consulted on White's proposition, discouraged the public approach and indicated his preference for Canadian borrowers to "employ the normal channels of relief."[37] Such a view was understandable enough, since Morgan's would reap the benefit of higher private interest rates and turn a handsome commission besides. McAdoo approved White's request in July.[38]

While White successfully plied McAdoo on the loan issue, Lord Reading brought the second point in Anglo-American-Canadian negotiations to a successful conclusion. He persuaded the Treasury Secretary in September to have U.S. loans to Great Britain include $15 million per month to pay for the American raw materials and components which entered Canada's British munitions production. This was in effect indirect U.S. aid to Canada, although the British had to be responsible for the bill.[39]

Such were the general and more immediate contexts from which the IMB-Ordnance Department agreement emerged in November, 1917. British compromises and Lord Reading's successful Washington mission smoothed the way in the higher reaches of politics. And a decline in British war orders coupled with mounting trade deficits with the United States increased Ottawa's desperation for a deal.

Representatives of the British War Mission and the IMB made their case to Ordnance Department officials that fall, and with good effect. Initiative rested primarily with the U.K.'s Washington Mission, for its staff was closer to the centers of both British and American officialdom. R. H. Brand of the Mission spoke with the Ordnance Department in early October. "Colonel Hoffer was anxious to have a full statement of the Canadian position and possibilities," he informed Flavelle, "with any remarks thereon that the Board would like to make."[40] Though pessimistic about the outcome at this point in time, Brand nevertheless suggested he could have Lord Northcliffe, the Mission chief, forward Flavelle's statement formally to the U.S. Government. In the meantime, Flavelle kept the Munitions Ministry in London informed of the Washington discussions.[41]

The pace of the talks quickened in mid-October. "Ordnance Department have today asked us urgently for statement of our unfilled capacity," the Mission's C. B. Gordon wired Flavelle on October 16, "asking for a list of firms and their capacity. We think Ordnance Department now ready to deal with that matter definitely."[42] At Gordon's request Flavelle immediately sent technical experts to Washington.

For the next few days Gordon, Brand and the IMB representatives discussed munitions production, with Ordnance officials underscoring the point that Canada's unused capacity could make a real contribution to the U.S. armament program.[43] They transmitted as well Flavelle's offer to have the IMB supervise any future orders. "If the United States authorities will give contracts . . . we would cheerfully supervise the production as though they were our own," he informed Gordon. "If they will do this, and you think it will be of any advantage, we will take as much pains with the output as if they were our own, charging them the bare cost of the service."[44]

By the first week of November the Canadian offer had been thoroughly analyzed and finally accepted. General Crozier, Chief of the Ordnance Department, offered Flavelle his compliments "on the closing of this mutually satisfactory and advantageous arrangement." It was, in Crozier's opinion, "a large job handled with astonishing expedition."[45]

Canadian business circles shared General Crozier's enthusiasm. The *Financial Post* regarded the Washington discussions of early November as "the most improtant development of the past three months."[46] That the Canadian government did not have to advance financial credits for this work, as it did in the case of British orders, heightened the attractiveness of the arrangment. Indeed the contribution the agreement could make to Canada's trade deficits with the U.S. was just the feature which appealed so much to the Borden Government. "It is of great importance having regard to the adverse trade balance," the Prime Minister remarked somewhat later, "that these orders should be placed as largely as possible."[47] Though rather self-conscious about what he had embarked upon while chairman of an imperial organization, Flavelle was nonetheless optimistic and hopeful. "It is most fortunate," he said in April, 1918, "that the American programme, in part at least, supplies the deficiency created by these and previous cancellations of the production of shells in Canada."[48] And to another correspondent he remarked, "all this means good money coming into the country and continued activity in many factories."[49] Canadian officials attached great importance to the agreement, and with good reason, for they expected contributions on several fronts.

The bonanza, however, turned out to be less than predicted. The flow of contracts grew only slowly in subsequent months. Flavelle estimated the IMB had completed about $56 million worth of orders under the agreement by May, 1918. He noted, though, that in comparing this production with British business one had to add roughly eighty percent to the value, "as in British business we included steel and all components, while in the American business the steel and components are supplied by the United States."[50] A month later he estimated that the aggregate value of the orders approached the $100 million mark.[51] More importantly he believed that half of the roughly $400 million worth of munitions business expected for 1919 would be U.S.-bound, a very significant observation indeed.[52] But according to the IMB's final report, however, of the roughly $178.4 million worth of orders placed only $32.8 million was paid for actual deliveries.[53] The IMB in contrast has spent as much as $1 million a day on British business in the peak months and had secured about $1 billion of contracts in all. Had the war continued, Flavelle's projections would probably have materialized, and certainly the trend was a growing one. But for the year during which the agreement actually ran, ultimate payment seemed to belie official optimism.

Administration of the agreement, moreover, was not without its difficulties. On February 25, 1918, Sir Robert Borden himself went to Washington for talks on, among other things, Canada's trade balance with the United States and the exchange situation. Lloyd Harris, head of the Canadian War Mission, told him that the "Americans unwilling to use facilities of Canada and want to pull everything over to [the] U.S.",[54] and there were similar gloomy assessments from other British and Canadian officials the next day. Everything seemed to hinge on Borden's meeting with Wilson on February 27th, a conversation that ended successfully when the President agreed that U.S. war orders should go to Canada. Bernard Baruch of the War Industries Board and Secretary McAdoo were similarly cooperative. On his return, Borden wrote that the Americans had "expressed the view that the resources of the two countries should be pooled in the most effective co-operation and that the boundary line had little or no significance in considering or dealing with these vital questions."[55] The war had made economic cooperation across the 49th parallel essential, and Borden, the leader of the fight against reciprocity in 1911, does not seem to have recalled his earlier worries about U.S. influence.

Flavelle, however, was never altogether comfortable with the requirements of the new relationship, conscious as he was of his primary obligation to the Ministry of Munitions. "Technically," he wrote to the head of the Canadian War Mission in Washington,

> we are a Department of the Ministry of Munitions. Our interest in Canadian Manufacturers technically, is to negotiate contracts for the production of munitions and other supplies needed by the Imperial Government in Canada. The only reason we can give the Ministry for the responsibility we have assumed for the Ordnance Department in Washington is, that by reason of having some voice in what is done for the Ordnance Department in Canada, we are better able to further the interests of the Ministry in the business which we are directed to place for them in Canada. There is no point where technically we have authority or responsibility to secure business for Canadian Manufacturers. . . . The practical position is — that because we are Canadians and deeply interested in everything that affects Canada, we are unable to hold ourselves exclusively to our technical position.[56]

He found it necessary, furthermore, to balance his secondary obligations to the Ordnance Department with mounting pressure from his Washington lobbyists to have the IMB assist the northward movement of contracts from yet additional U.S. government departments. "Back of every other consideration," he instructed Canada's Mission chief, "I am sure you will always bear in mind and help your officers to keep before them that our primary duty is not to find business for the Canadian manufacturers; that the primary duty is to keep ourselves strong to meet the necessitous requirements associated first with the British business, and second, with this newly acquired American business."[57]

At the same time Flavelle complained of the Ordnance Department's habit of offering higher prices on contracts negotiated directly than those offered through the agency of the IMB. Canadian businessmen, conversely, complained that the Board sometimes vetoed contracts personally promised them by Ordnance officials. Aware of the political implications of such criticism, Flavelle alerted Borden to the problem:

> Manufacturers from Canada who visit Washington, and who meet now one set of officers and again another, carry away assurances that contracts will be given them. They wait on us in Ottawa and feel raw and sore because we are without definite instructions from Washington that we may place further orders. Others go to Washington and secure promises for very important quantities of shells; they are sent to us, when we find — either from our previous experience with them, or because they give no evidence of having made a careful study of what they have promised to do — we are unable to recommend contract [sic] to be placed, except for a greatly reduced quantity. This causes irritation and the whole circle of their friends are affected.[58]

There were difficulties for Flavelle's Washington contacts as well. Criticism from Canadian business interests annoyed them, as did Flavelle's obvious restraint in responding to additional orders.[59] They were far more acutely aware of the strenuousness of the competition for American contracts, and sensitive too to the sentiment among some U.S. officials against letting good business leave the country. Lloyd Harris, chairman of the Canadian War Mission, warned Flavelle at one point: "In discussing our activities here with Sir Robert Borden in Newyork [sic] on saturday [sic], I suggest that results being obtained in securing business should not be made public as we think effect of publicity would be detrimental at the present time."[60]

The most difficult and exasperating chore of all,

however, came with the war's end, as the IMB and Canadian manufacturers confronted the avalanche of contract cancellations. Alarm in October, 1918, became despair in November. Since so many U.S. orders had been given informally the contractors had no legal recourse for payment. Flavelle gamely tried to advance the principle that cancellations should fall first on manufacturers in the U.S., a naive hope at best.[61] Settling Canadian claims in Washington dragged on into late 1919. "In many cases," commented Flavelle, "it has been the most disagreeable task we have had to perform."[62]

The IMB-Ordnance Department agreement did not in the end displace British munitions as the major source of IMB business, though it might very well have begun to rival it had the war continued through 1919. Nor did the agreement solve the country's perennial balance of trade and exchange problems with the U.S. These issues continued to take Sir Thomas White to Washington, just as mounting British adversity stimulated additional Victory Loans at home. In retrospect the Ordnance Department-IMB agreement is more important as a symbol of broader trends and patterns of the war years than as an instrument of practical accomplishment.

As a window into the nature of Canada's relationships with both Britain and the United States the agreement is significant indeed. For one thing it shows how the Canadian search for American business arose in large part out of the difficulties in Anglo-Canadian economics. In the Ordnance Department-IMB agreement we can see that any "pull" from the south was more than matched by that "push" from across the Atlantic. The same dynamic characterizes the actions of Sir Thomas White as well. He turned reluctantly to U.S. money markets in 1915, and he remained anxious to avoid a direct U.S. government loan as late as 1917. At the same time the agreement nevertheless exemplifies very well how Flavelle and White hoped to reduce their problems both with the British and on the home front through special arrangements with the United States. From this perspective, we can see that Canadian officials turned to the United States as a safety valve to release imperial and domestic pressures. Both men intended to increase their freedom of action by access to U.S. funds.[63]

To this extent the Canadians simply joined the Allies in turning to American economic resources as the war crisis deepened. Canada shared in North American prosperity with the U.S., but it suffered a double dependency. Prosperity followed European war orders in both Canada and the United States, but from the beginning Canada depended in large part upon U.S. supplies to fill them. Canada's increased adverse trade balance with the United States exemplified this economic fact of life. As the drain on British resources intensified, Ottawa could no longer redress this balance with her surplus with London. Some kind of arrangement became essential, therefore, over and above other measures which might be taken, such as controlling U.S. imports.

In contrast to the tense and sometimes hard negotiations with the British, Canadian relations with American officals went relatively smoothly. The role of personal relations was especially important for Sir Thomas White, for he had to deal with Treasury Secretary McAdoo, a man who had proven so troublesome to British representatives in the summer of 1917. White worked hard to cultivate friendly relations with his U.S. counterpart. Both during and after the crisis of 1917 his requests were as personal as they were informal. Whether by luck or by design he displayed the kind of deference and respect required to win McAdoo's favor. Anxious to create a common bond, White built a bridge to McAdoo along the lines of two finance ministers faced with similar questions who could understand and sympathize with each other's problems. In enlisting McAdoo's sympathy at one point, White offered what might be considereda classic statement of the good neighbor approach to Canadian-American relations.

> We have in your time and my time always been good neighbors. Occasionally a verbal brickbat has been thrown across the fence but we have always sympathized with each other when brickbats have come from any foreign source. In our attitude towards constitutional liberty and all social problems our peoples are very much alike and understand each other better I think than any other two peoples in the world today. The struggle in a common cause will I am sure greatly cement our friendship and respect for each other.[64]

In contrast to White, Flavelle's was a more bureaucratic and prosaic task, administering an agreement which had been worked out largely among the technical staffs of the IMB and Ordnance Department. But of course the success of even this enterprise was obviously conditioned by the kind of personal good will which Sir Thomas for one so studiously cultivated.

The Ordnance Department-IMB agreement occupied only a small place in Canada's total economic effort during the Great War. Canadian war prosperity certainly did not rest upon it. It was nevertheless indicative of important trends running through the tangled web of wartime relationships. Above all, it was, in retrospect, a signal of the future. It not only presaged continuous Canadian efforts in the twentieth century to crack the U.S. defence market on behalf of domestic prosperity, but it also symbolized very well the continental element in the Canadian response to international crisis.

CHAPTER THREE

LLOYD HARRIS AND THE CANADIAN
WAR MISSION TO WASHINGTON

The Canadian government formally established a War Mission in Washington, D.C. on 2 February, 1918. There were precedents for the Canadian Mission. Major delegations of statesmen and technicians arrived from the major Allied countries immediately after American entry into the war in April, 1917, and more permanent Missions soon followed. The Balfour Mission had arrived from England in April, for example, and Canadian officials were soon added to its entourage.[1] An independent Canadian Mission, in contrast, took comparatively longer to crystallize.

Why was this so? There are two points to bear in mind in answering this question. First of all there were the strong ties that bound Canada so securely to empire. Within the ideology of Canadian officialdom there was precious little room for any sentiment of genuine independence. Canadian nationalism, such as it was, found its outlet in a romantic imperialism. Diplomatic and economic conerns helped to sustain a psychology of colonialism. Britain's Washington embassy traditionally administered Canada's relations with the United States, though it was superseded in these tasks after 1917 by such emergency agencies as the British War Mission. Most telling of all, of course, was the popular view that Canada was at war because Britain was at war. Some advanced nationalists argued differently but the man on the street was probably correct: Canada *was* at war because Britain was.

The economic ties of empire were equally strong. Reciprocity in 1911 had been defeated in large part because of the sentimental – and financial – attachment to them. Britain received tariff preferences in Canada, and Britain was Canada's largest foreign market. London still was the finance capital of the world, and virtually all Canadian loans, public and private, were floated there. And British investment in Canada was enormous, amounting in 1914 to seventy-two percent of the total foreign investment in the Dominion, a sum of $2278 million.[2] The immediate impact of the war was to intensify these links and to make their preservation even more of an emotional matter than they had been.

But in addition to the imperial channels to U.S. officialdom, Canada also possessed her own Washington contacts, and their value should not be overlooked. The comparatively slow emergence of a Canadian War Mission is owed in part to their very effectiveness. These included the traditional journeys to Washington of Sir Joseph Pope, the Under Secretary of State for External Affairs. Pope had been an important Canadian element in negotiations within the "Atlantic triangle" ever since the formation of Canada's Department of External Affairs in 1909. Canadian cabinet ministers occasionally made the southerly trek as well, as did the Prime Minister, Sir Robert Borden. Canada's proximity to the United States permitted an unusual entrée to Washington officials outside the regular routes of access through British channels.[3]

In the early war years the two traditional paths to Washington seemed adequate enough. To be sure, the case

could always be made for permanent Canadian representation on constitutional grounds, and Sir Robert
Borden was ready to advocate this point of view after
1914. Novel economic problems emerged as well as the
war progressed, but regular market mechanisms seemed
sufficient to take care of most of them. Those which
transcended the market usually yielded to the good offices
of the British ambassador, Sir Cecil Spring-Rice, and
Pope's periodic visits.

But American entry into the war transformed the
dynamics of Canadian-U.S. relations. A welter of Washington agencies sprang into action. Controls extended
rapidly over large sectors of the American economy. The
free market gave way to a putative state capitalism.[4] U.S.
government buyers joined Allied purchasers and regular
domestic customers in the competition for scarce resources. Economic concerns reinforced traditional constitutional arguments for Canadian representation after
April, 1917 and practical necessities challenged constitutional scruples.

References to coal and steel, priority regulations, and
food controls insinuated themselves on the memoranda
which guided Sir Joseph Pope in his increasing number of
trips across the border in the months after April, 1917. An
army of U.S. emergency administrators complicated his
task further. Pope now had to add the names of such
people as Bernard Baruch of the Council of National
Defence (CND), Herbert Hoover of the Food Administration, and Robert Lovett of the War Industries Board
(WIB) to his list of regular contacts in the federal
government departments. The new administrators, moreover, demanded specialized information and comprehensive statistics on Canadian needs which were well
beyond Pope's competence or range. They urged upon him
as well various forms of technical coordination, proposals

which required an expert response. "I saw Mr. Hoover, the Food Controller," Pope noted at one point, "And asked him how far Canada could co-operate with them in the matter of food control. He replied that, in his judgment, not merely co-operation but identic action on the part of Canada was essential to the task he had in hand."[5] Somewhat later on the same visit Pope spoke with the Assistant Secretary of the Navy, Franklin Roosevelt. "He stated that the United States Government was of the opinion that the whole coast defence of the continent should be a matter of common conern to both countries; that we should, as it were, pool our defensive resources."[6]

Nor were the new administrators as open to the personal, informal appeal that Pope had used with such good affect on his old contacts in the State Department. On one occasion in mid-September, 1917, for instance, Pope appealed to the WIB's Priority Committee to place the Canadian Car and Foundry Company on its preference list for steel requirements. This was a particularly important matter for Pope, because the Prime Minister had personally intervened on behalf of a request from company president Senator Curry. But Robert Lovett's Priority Committee turned Pope down flat. The Under Secretary reverted to his friends at State in a typical Canadian appeal:

> I said that Judge Lovett's decision, however reasonable it might be, was based altogether on commercial grounds, and that I ventured to think the case might be reviewed also from a somewhat higher plane; that is to say, as a direct request of one Government to another, in the consideration of which it seemed to me reasons of international comity should have some weight. I said that we, on our part, had always accorded special consideration to requests emanating directly from the United States Government, and that I still ventured to hope that some way might be found of meeting the desires of the Canadian Government in this case, particularly in view of the

fact of the two Governments being Allies, as it were, partners in a common cause.[7]

Clearly Canada could no longer depend on sympathy and informality alone. It needed to marshal evidence and specialized knowledge to make its case among the Washington businessmen bureaucrats. From this perspective the Canadian War Mission of February, 1918 simply exemplifies the bureaucratic trends of war, as informal arrangements gave way to formal rules and specialized expertise supplemented sentiment in economic negotiations.

Sir Joseph Flavelle, head of the Imperial Munitions Board (IMB), like his counterpart at External, found his Washington contacts unable to guarantee Canadian interests in the spring and summer of 1917. Indeed, his friends at the British War Mission readily admitted that they had neither the information nor the time to do justice to Canadian requests. The Vice-Chairman of the War Mission, C. B. Gordon, was acutely aware of the deficiencies. A Canadian businessman, and Flavelle's former colleague at the IMB, Gordon did what he could to protect the IMB's interests, and he acted as Flavelle's middleman with the American bureaucracy. He did for Canadian interests on one level what Sir Joseph Pope was trying simultaneously to do on another. Gordon tunneled through a British administrative unit while Pope stayed with his own techniques. No formal Canadian mechanism existed, in other words, through which these kinds of requests could be channeled. Gordon, in the meantime, responded to inquisitive U.S. administrators. He countered WIB arguments over the price of steel supplies, for example, and he negotiated with the Allied Purchasing Commision over the status of Canadian purchases. Gordon also shared Flavelle's mounting anxiety over British cutbacks in Canadian purchases during the summer and fall of 1917, and made inquiries about defence contracts with the American War Department.[8]

Flavelle and his IMB officials also made the rounds in Washington during these months. In April, for example, Flavelle personally spoke with the first chairman of the WIB, Frank A. Scott, a Cleveland manufacturer. In this instance, he received encouraging reports on the future of U.S. supplies of copper, lead and brass.[9] In the following months Flavelle also dispatched his assistant, Edward Fitzgerald, a former purchasing officer with the Canadian Pacific Railroad, to meet Bernard Baruch and his men on the CND's Raw Materials Committee.[10] But the IMB chief recognized that neither Gordon's efforts nor periodic personal visits could solve his problems. As early as May, therefore, he favoured the idea of a permanent IMB representative, and he continued to press this proposal in subsequent months.[11]

Flavelle's Washington friends could not object. R. H. Brand, financial advisor to the British War Mission, felt the situation was particularly urgent for Canada since American regulations and controls would only become more stringent as the crisis deepened.

> As the United States Government are forced to control industry, fix prices, regulate priority, etc., etc., so they are going to ask more and more whether the Canadian Government are doing the same thing, whether they or the British Government are limiting domestic consumption, and whether they are purchasing to the full for war purposes the war materials which the Canadian plants are capable of turning out.[12]

It was just this kind of sentiment that Sir Joseph Pope would encounter before the WIB's Priority Committee. "People connected with the War Industries Board come to us daily," said Brand, "and want assurances from us that we are utilizing to the full, Canadian supplies. They ask why, when shell steel is so very difficult to get here, we should come and get large supplies here, if we are not using our Canadian capacity to the full."[13] Again, as Sir Joseph Pope discovered, only detailed information would satisfy sceptical U.S. officials. Members of the British War Mission, of course, could not always produce it. Nor did they have time to do so. Brand warned Flavelle in early October that "We do not want to have to endorse all the Canadian requests for priority, nor are we in a position to do so, and the only alternative that I can see is for the Canadian Government to set up their own organization, either in conjunction with us here, or entirely separate."[14]

For Flavelle, moreover, the whole issue of attracting U.S. defence orders to Canada became crucial in the late summer of 1917 so he was all the more anxious that the IMB establish a Washington office "with a competent officer and staff."[15] Such a group could relieve the British War Mission of the details of Canadian business.

Other Ottawa officials pressed the idea of Canadian representation in Washington on Borden in the fall of 1917. C. A. Magrath, the Fuel Controller, who had his own continuing problems in Washington, spoke with the Prime Minister about the idea of a special Washington representative in early September. His recommendation, very close to the final arrangement, is worth quoting in full.

> To a very large extent the new problems that are being grappled with at Washington are also our problems. The interests of the two countries are interwoven as they never were before. It is therefore of the utmost importance that Canada should have at Washington a man of exceptional ability to represent her. He must be a big enough man to hold up Canada's interests with the exceptional men who are now directing affairs at Washington. He must also have such a status as will ensure him a hearing at any time. The only practicable plan, it seems to me, is to secure the right man, and send him to Washington immediately, as the direct representative of the

Prime Minister. Under ordinary circumstances it would be most undesirable to have a representative of Canada in Washington independent of the British Embassy, but these are abnormal times and demand special remedies.[16]

Sir Robert Borden had not been inactive in the cause of Canadian representation in Washington. He had raised the point early in the war and pressed the case with much greater intensity after April, 1917. But opposition in London to a Canadian representative independent of the British Embassy blocked a speedy resolution of the problem. Such an idea, to quote the Colonial Secretary, raised a "grave constitutional question."[17]

In pressing his case for diplomatic representation that fall, Borden drew some of his best arguments from the war experience itself. In a late October wire to London he argued that

> At present Canadian Food Controller, Canadian Fuel Controller and Canadian Board of Grain Supervisors confer directly with corresponding Boards in United States, and quick and efficient co-operation is thereby secured. To these methods of procedure I am not aware that any constitutional objections have been or can be urged. They have developed naturally by ignoring old forms which have lost their meaning and adopting direct and businesslike means of communication.[18]

Borden assured British officials that "there is no desire to create anything in the nature of a separate Embassy."[19] London, however, remained restive into the winter of 1917-1918, and there the controversy rested as Borden plunged into the more urgent problems of constructing a Union Government.[20]

Flavelle and the IMB, however, could not wait for the resolution of the constitutional issue. Their developing agreement for defence contracts with the U.S. Army's Ordnance Department made action all the more imperative. By late October Flavelle had decided that a

Canadian representative of the IMB in Washington was mandatory, and he so informed Sir Robert Borden.[21] Flavelle then turned to Lloyd Harris. He could not have made a better choice.

Of a farm machinery family in Brantford, Harris was described by one contemporary as "a clever, capable man of large affairs; he is an ardent Canadian, and a strong believer in Canada's ever growing importance in the Empire."[22] Active in a number of business enterprises in the pre-war years, Harris had been instrumental in the merger of several steel manufacuring plants in Ontario and in the subsequent formation of the Steel Company of Canada.[23] Moreover, as the former Liberal MP from Brantford, he had already gained public prominence as one of the leaders of the Liberal revolt against reciprocity in 1911. Indeed, in company with Clifford Sifton, Zebulon Lash and J. S. Willison, Harris had visited Borden personally in that election year to exact the Liberal dissidents' price for their support. And the demands, revealing of Harris's outlook, included a reorganization of the Department of Trade and Commerce, and the establishment of a commercial consular service "in order to protect Canadian interests and expand Canadian trade."[24] Harris would never lose sight of these goals throughout his Washington adventure.

When Canada entered the Great War, Harris and his firm, the Russell Motor Car Company, moved into the munitions business with contracts from the Canadian Shell Committee. This Committee, composed of private manufacturers, had been established by the Minister of Militia, Sir Sam Hughes, in 1915. More orders followed from the IMB, and the profits of Russell and Company mounted accordingly. The *Financial Post* estimated that by late 1917 the Company's munitions department netted profits of $643,590.[25] Harris also had retained his interest in federal politics in the meantime. When Flavelle's call came, Harris was in the midst of meetings with Conservative Party officials, arranging Liberal Unionist constituencies for the forthcoming federal elections.[26]

Harris, then, brought a number of important qualifications to his new task. He had the best of political connections, as well as important personal experience in federal politics. He had, moreover, a wide experience in business as well as specialized knowledge of the new munitions industry. He was also accustomed to moving in that twilight zone between business and government, between private and public institutions, a characteristic of fundamental importance to his Washington war work. Indeed his negotiations with Borden in 1911 had exemplified a continuing theme of his career both in peace and in war: he intended to bend the state to the support and protection of Canadian economic expansion. During his Washington sojourn, as before, Harris would combine public position and private skill on behalf of national economic development. His experience in this endeavour, in turn, would have an influential bearing on the emergence of the Canadian War Mission in February, 1918.

By mid-November Harris had begun to make the rounds in Washington with letters of introduction from Flavelle to a bevy of U.S. officials. He spoke to Baruch and Baruch's steel expert, Leonard Replogle, "and I was able to place before these two men, our Canadian situation and to urge upon them the necessity of the United States adopting a pretty liberal policy towards Canada at the present time."[27] He pressed Ordnance officials to utilize Canadian production facilities. "I know that our Manufacturers are anxious for business of this kind," he wrote Flavelle in one instance, "and if a good volume of business can be secured, it will give a lot of employment, and enable our people to keep their organization intact."[28] He also had to construct his own organization. "I have been pretty badly handicapped since my arrival on account of the lack of staff," he wrote Sir Joseph at the end of November, "but this will be remedied from now on."[29] Then, too, he had to adjust his activities to suit both the IMB's American Department and the British War Mission's routines. And all the while Canadian business representatives drew him and his staff into service along the U.S. contract trail.[30]

Though ostensibly a representative of the IMB and the Munitions Ministry in London, Harris functioned essentially as a lobbyist for Canadian manufacturers. Flavelle was rather sensitive about the ambiguity of Harris's activities in this regard and cautioned him more than once to restrain the crusade for American war orders. The IMB, after all, owed its chief allegiance to the British Ministry of Munitions.[31] But Harris remained the unabashed enthusiast. He picked up the tasks that had so beleaguered Sir Joseph Pope, and which had fallen to Gordon and Brand at the British War Mission. These included such things as speeding up shipments of U.S. spare parts to Canada, seeking exemptions for Canadian buyers from various kinds of U.S. controls, and gaining the requisite priority orders for Canadian-bound goods. There were discouragements, of course, and a great deal of wrangling with the emergency agencies. But Harris never lost his optimism. Sir Robert Borden spoke with him and others of his staff in Washington in early January as he returned from one of his periodic visits to Hot Springs, Georgia. "They say much has been done in acquainting Am. Gov't. with Canada's equipment for producing munitions," he noted in his diary, "and with good results. They think great opportunity ahead of us."[32]

Harris's chief handicap was a lack of formal authority, a deficiency which not even his enthusiasm and persistence could overcome. Two months in Washington convinced him, in fact, that Canada required far stronger representation. He took his case to Borden in mid-January. Citing the example of the other Allied war missions, Harris urged the Prime Minister to appoint a Canadian counterpart "for the purpose of looking after Canadian interests and needs, and also in securing favourable consideration from the United States Government in their dealings with Canada at the present time on all trade matters."[33] What Harris had in mind was simply the formal recognition and extension of the organization he already had under construction. He wanted it differentiated from the IMB and British officialdom and given independent status. He recommended, therefore, that the head of a Canadian War Mission "be clothed with sufficient authority, and given a standing which would entitle him to be kept informed on all financial negotiations" among the Canadian, British and the U.S. governments.[34] Harris wanted Canada to have a standing equivalent to the missions of the other allied countries in wartime Washington.

Harris's intervention with Borden in mid-January could not have come at a more strategic time. The Prime Minister had already informed British officials of his intention to take up the issue of Canadian permanent representation once again after the election in December, 1917. A resounding Union victory strengthened his resolve. Harris's proposal, moreover, carried special weight as the culmination of two months of personal experience with the bureaucratic battles of wartime Washington, and it came from a man whose judgment Borden had every reason to respect.

Even if the Prime Minister had never considered the problem of Canada's Washington representation before January, there is every reason to think he would have responded to Harris's appeal. And this is an important point. For it means that an appreciation of the economics of Canadian-American relations is far more important in understanding the origins and operations of the Canadian War Mission than prior debates over the constitutional principles of Anglo-Canadian relations. The Canadian War Mission, an emergency measure, was designed to strengthen Canada's position in the political economy of war. As Borden emphasized in his cables to British officials, Canadian desire for independence of empire was not the point at issue, not at all.

Borden had Loring Christie, his legal counsel, draw up a draft of the mission's charter and then dispatched him to Washington to consult with Harris and British officials. Christie spoke with Harris both before and after going to the British embassy. Harris was "entirely satisfied with the terms of the draft," Christie reported, though he did make a few simple alterations. For one thing he had Christie add a paragraph giving the Mission chairman the right to recommend additional members for appointment by the Governor-in-Council. "Mr. Harris had it in mind to ask a number of prominent Canadian businessmen to go to Washington to assist him in various aspects of the work," Christie informed Borden, "and as they would give their service without pay, he thought such a paragraph would be useful as giving them a certain status and so making it easier to ask them to join him." Harris also combined with R. H. Brand of the British War Mission to draw up a paragraph on the desirability of general cooperation between the two missions.[35]

The charter of the Canadian War Mission was designed to secure Lloyd Harris's services. Clearly it answered his appeal to Borden for authority and status. By the order in council creating the War Mission (P. C. 272 of 2 Feb., 1918), the Mission chairman would be "empowered to represent the Cabinet and the heads of the various Departments and other administrative branches of the

Government . . . in respect of negotiations relating to purely Canadian affairs." He would in addition exercise general oversight of the activities of all Canadian government officials stationed in the United States. Though his mission would act "in the closest conjunction" with its British counterpart, the chairman was not subordinate to it. On the contrary, "On questions of importance arising directly out of his Mission" he would report directly to the Prime Minister. Moreover, he was "entitled to be informed on all negotiations between His Majesty's Government and the Government of the United States in so far as they affect Canada." He was empowered as well "under special direction from the Prime Minister and in complete conjunction with His Majesty's High Commissioner and Special Ambassador at Washington, to engage in negotiations with the Government of the United States relating to affairs which, while directly concerning Canada, may also affect the interests of the British Commonwealth as a whole."[36] Harris could not have asked for more.

His appointment as chairman of the Canadian War Mission hardly came as a surprise. His recommendations, after all, were vitally important to the Mission's ultimate design, and no other name seems to have been considered during the entire discussions. Nor could Harris be expected to refuse a position so aptly suited to his grand ambitions. "I congratulate the country upon having secured your services in this most important position," the Prime Minister wrote him on 1 February, 1918, "and I am confident that your work will prove to be of immense advantage to Canadian interests."[37] Harris pledged in return to "do my best for Canada."[38]

The Mission received an allotment of $150,000 from the budget of the Department of External Affairs, and its staff increased substantially in subsequent months. Several businessmen joined Harris as planned, including R. H.

McMaster of the Steel Company of Canada and Frank A. Rolph of a Toronto printing firm, and they were supported by a staff of 34 by mid-May.[39] The Mission's activities, though diverse, were all directed to the central goal of extending and protecting Canada's economic interests. Mission members lobbied for contracts; they negotiated with Washington bureaucrats for supplies of crucial raw materials; they advised Ottawa in the tactics of response to a bewildering proliferation of government regulations; and they guided visiting Canadian businessmen through the labyrinth of Washington officialdom. In sum, the Mission attempted to arrange an advantageous coordination of economic policies across the 49th parallel.

Throughout these activities Harris reported directly to the Prime Minister and enjoyed his full support. With a direct wire service to Ottawa, the Mission fulfilled some of the functions of an embassy, although as an extension of the inner circle of Canadian policy makers, it was something more. It stood as a distinct and independent unit, though it did cooperate with its counterpart, the British War Mission, and with the British Embassy. For its part, the Wilson administration was favourably disposed towards the Mission's creation. President Wilson informed Borden in February of his hope that the direct wire service between Washington and Ottawa "will contribute still further to promote a good understanding and lasting friendship between Canada and the United States."[40]

In one sense, the Mission's formation simply allowed Lloyd Harris to extend his efforts on behalf of Canadian business, the goal which brought him to Washington in the first place. In functional terms the Canadian War Mission had begun in November, 1917. But its emergence also touched on larger themes. It was an explicit recognition of the inability of Canadian business interests to find adequate representation through imperial diplomatic channels, and it illustrated how the growth of economic activity across the 49th parallel simply overflowed the bounds of existing Anglo-Canadian organization. The Canadian War Mission was simply one example of the inevitable process of differentiation which occurred among Canadian and British organizations in several areas of the war effort.

The Mission was also a significant example of the shift in the economic center of gravity in the United States from New York to Washington after April, 1917. Until that time, centers of private economic power, of which New York was the symbol, were uppermost, and the traditional patterns of communication with them had sufficed. But American belligerent status had changed all that. "Washington," C. B. Gordon told Flavelle, "is the centre of all activity at present, and you might as well try to do business in Glasgow with the Government of Great Britain, as to try to do business in New York with the Government of the United States."[41] Though by no means entirely superseded, private centers of economic power had at least to share the stage with Washington and with public officials. Canadian buyers, for example, had now to go through the central government to reach private American business. The Canadian War Mission, it was hoped, could give them a better entrée.

From a broader perspective yet, the shift of power to the United States and to Washington may be seen as emphasizing as never before the imperative need to coordinate economic activity on a North American scale. Herbert Hoover, Bernard Baruch and other U.S. officials had suggested this to Sir Joseph Pope in the early months of U.S. belligerency. The constant growth of American controls emphasized this point of view even more. Canadians had now to take a more comprehensive look at their resources and needs if they were to make a better case for themselves before U.S. administrators. U.S. entry into the war, as the Privy Council report on the Canadian War Mission pointed out, made it desirable not only better to represent Dominion interests, but also to secure "the most effective cooperation between Canada and the United States in respect of many economic and financial measures vitally connected with the prosecution of the war."[42] And as F. P. Jones of the Ottawa War Trade Board put it to the Prime Minister in January, 1918,

> The seriousness of the present war situation makes it incumbent that every resource of both countries be used to the best possible advantage for the prosecution of the war. Materials should therefore be allocated to firms and factories who can make most efficient use of them for the prosecution of the war irrespective of the origin of the materials, or in which country the plant is located. Arrangements should be made [to] ... coordinate priority and licensing arrangements so as to bring about the above results with the least possible delay.[43]

The war had made forms of economic continentalism a necessity, and it is not inconceivable that if the war had lasted into 1919 and beyond that an integration comparable to that of the Second World War would have resulted.

Lloyd Harris and his Mission also became mediators of U.S.-Canadian economic relations as well as promoters for Canadian business enterprise. Harris, like Gordon and Pope before him, became a middleman between U.S. and Canadian officialdom. He had to convince American bureaucrats of the legitimacy of Canadian requests while at the same time he sought Canadian policies which would appease U.S. officials. His work and the work of the Mission was a microcosm of the continental current in Canadian wartime economic policy. Harris's nationalism, which was real enough, necessarily took on a continentalist hue.

Harris had considerable success in his role as coordinator, and by comparison with the friction between London and Ottawa, U.S.-Canadian economic relations proceeded remarkably smoothly throughout the war. This goodwill was hardly owed solely to Harris and his Mission, of course. The Mission, after all, could hardly supervise all economic interactions across the 49th parallel despite its formal authorization to do so. Other government departments and war boards maintained their own contacts and conducted their own negotiations; and Sir Thomas White and Sir Robert Borden, among Cabinet officials, made Washington visits. Private businessmen, moreover, could not always be persuaded to work through the Mission, and they sometimes insisted on dealing with U.S. officials on a direct basis. Furthermore, Harris had to work within broader Canadian policies on such economic issues as the balance of payments and energy policy which were well beyond his control. There were, as well, broader economic features of a structural kind which necessarily set constraints on his freedom of action. Canada depended upon the United States for half her coal and even more of her steel supplies, after all, which naturally put Canada and Harris in a dependency relationship with American officials.

Debates over steel imports and energy policy can illustrate many of these general comments. These issues stood at the heart of Canadian-U.S. economics during the war, and Harris and his War Mission played a part in both of them.

The question of U.S. steel supplies occupied a particularly important place in Canadian thinking from the earliest days of U.S. belligerency. Pig iron, ferro silicone, alloy steel, boiler plates and various kinds of wire were all vital to munitions output, and all derived to a greater or lesser extent from American sources. Certainly, the insufficiency had been recognized well before 1917, but no

effective policies had emerged to alleviate it. The consequences became crystal clear as the United States began
to conserve supplies for her own purposes in the summer
and fall of 1917. The squeeze on Canadian buyers
tightened as the WIB established priorities and the War
Trade Board inaugurated a programme of export licensing.
Canadian importers pressured the Trade and Commerce
Department for action throughout the summer, and an
advisory committee of steelmen appeared in September.
But the anxiety remained. A great transportation tie-up in
the United States during the winter of 1917-1918 only
compounded the difficulties, and Canadian importers
raised cries for a "steel controller" to administer increasingly scarce imports. By late January, despite repeated
appeals to the U.S. War Trade Board, the future of steel
imports remained uncertain.[44]

Harris shared the pervasive gloom among Canadian
officials that winter. He was more sensitive than most,
however, to some of the reasons behind American reluctance to sanction steel exports. The psychology of the War
Trade Board, he realized, was especially dangerous. The
Board believed that Canadian buyers took advantage of
fixed American prices to purchase at lower prices in the
United States than were available to them in Canada. The
Board supported its case by claiming that some Canadian
pig iron producers had personally asked the Board to hold
up export applications so as to head off those Canadian
buyers who were trying to get out of older and more
expensive Canadian contracts. Responding to the situation,
Harris urged his government to make a comprehensive
survey of total Canadian requirements so that he could
effectively deal with American officials. He urged as well
that Canada fix the price of pig iron to eliminate the
apprehension among American officials over the price
differential. In other words, the solution lay in part in

bringing Canadian and American regulations into line. No theme was to be more characteristic of Harris's work throughout 1918.[45]

With the Canadian War Mission firmly established, Harris stepped up pressure on U.S. officials after Feburary, 1918, and with some success. Through his good offices, for example, Canada received in the last half of June, 1918 1,500 tons per week of ship plates and 100 tons per week of locomotive steel.[46] By this time the Mission had gained rather favourable consideration, so much so that R. H. McMaster could write to the War Trade Board in May, 1918:

> We have alway been met, by your Board, on the broad lines that favourable consideration would be given Canadian requirements for any material, the use of which was not prohibited in the United States and it has always been expected that, if supplies of pig iron or any other commodity were allowed for any purposes in the States, equal treatment would be granted Canadian needs for purposes of a similarly important character.[47]

So accustomed indeed had Canadians grown to this kind of arrangement that McMaster waxed indignant when Canadian munitions manufacturers suffered shortages while supplies were apparently available to American and Allied buyers. A brief which McMaster delivered to the War Trade Board on this point in the fall of 1918 aptly summarizes the arguments and justifications of the Canadian appeal:

> I believe you are mindful of the fact that Canada has been over four years at War and can claim distinction for what has been done, both Overseas and at home. You will also recall that, before the War, Canada was the second best customer of the United States. Her commercial conditions were, in many lines and particularly Iron and Steel, dependent upon supplies of American raw and finished materials, perhaps to a greater

degree than was good for the country. We have made many adjustments in our commercial conditions and plan to do more to make ourselves more self-supporting but you will realize that such changes cannot be accomplished by the stroke of a pen and time will be required. I believe, however, from the standpoint of our past trade that in proportion to our demands upon you, which have all been paid for in cash, no belligerent can come to this country for materials with better grace than Canada.[48]

Harris also intervened in power and fuel questions, first as a representative of the IMB and then as head of the War Mission, taking up his role as interpreter between Ottawa and Washington. It was in this capacity that Harris brought the American viewpoint to Canadian decision-making.

The power problem, an especially explosive issue, required the utmost delicacy. At issue here was the flow of hydro-electric energy from Niagara Falls to American munitions plants in northern New York State. The personality and goals of Sir Adam Beck of Ontario Hydro complicated the issue further. Throughout the war period, Beck intensified his drive to control the private power companies, hoping thereby to reduce substantially their power exports to the United States. In one attempt to head off Beck on this point, Borden instigated an investigation in the fall of 1917 under Sir Henry Drayton, and Drayton, as expected, recommended the continuation of exports to U.S. munitions plants. But cooperation from Beck was no more certain in subsequent months.[49]

Increasingly anxious about the question after April, 1917, American officials intervened with the Canadian government on behalf of their industrial clientele. Their investigations and reports dove-tailed with the federal inquiry. The WIB sent its power expert to Buffalo, Niagara Falls and Ottawa that fall. He noted the bad feeling between Beck's Hydro-Electric Commission and the private Canadian companies, and worried over Beck's request that Ottawa prohibit the exports of electricity from the private companies. Clearly siding with Ottawa in the matter, he cited Sir Henry Drayton's argument with approval and was pleased to find Borden and his ministers ready to cooperate. But the matter was not easily resolved.[50] Complaints from the American side continued as American officials urged additional supplies for plants in New York as well as for Ontario branch plants producing strategic materials.[51]

Harris did his best to mediate the dispute, but it was a very difficult task. There were problems with Canadian officials like Joseph Flavelle who remained skeptical as to whether American companies either in Canada or the United States used power exclusively for war purposes. Concerned as he was with Canadian munitions production for the British, Flavelle was wary of having scarce resources expended by U.S. plants for commercial purposes. He noted at one point: "It seems to me . . . a remarkable position for a United States official to seek to direct how this Power is to be supplied in Canada."[52] Harris, on the other hand, wanted Canada to impress American officials with its efforts to conserve power supplies. He wondered in January if Canada was doing enough: "It is believed here that while [U.S.] has secured results apparently the Canadian situation has not been improved. This will have an effect on Canadian coal situation unless immediate steps are taken to show that Canada is really doing something effective in diverting power from non-essential uses."[53]

The issue of electrical power and coal were intertwined. It was Harris's contention that if Canada did not provide power, Americans would withhold coal. There is no evidence that Harris threatened American officials with lack of power if Canada did not receive its coal or steel supplies, but there is evidence that American administrators assumed that Canadians would indeed use their control of hydro-electricity as a club in bargaining sessions. As WIB administrator Alexander Legge informed priorities commissioner Edwin Parker in February, 1918:

Generally speaking, I believe that we are likely to supply Canada with a larger portion of their steel when [sic] we have been furnishing during the past few months, partly for the reason that we wish them to release some power for the cyanamid plant and also for the Union Carbide plant whose production at present is greatly reduced because of the cutting off of power supplied from the Canadian side.[54]

In the face of continuing U.S. pressure, WIB officials even suggested that the British Forgings plant in Toronto should be shut down to release power for the use of the American Cyanamid Company of Niagara Falls and the Union Carbide Company of Welland, an interference which particularly irritated Flavelle.

The Canadian business community, in so far as the *Financial Post* is representative, favored Drayton and Borden over Beck and Ontario. It worried that if Beck had his way and cut off electricity to the United States, the United States would indeed retaliate by withholding coal supplies. It supported centralized control under the federal government of this particular issue.[55] Borden and the government shared the *Financial Post*'s sensitivity to American demands. "The Government has decided that these plants must be supplied," Newton Rowell ultimately informed Power Controller Sir Henry Drayton, "and it is desired that you should take whatever action may be necessary to insure that this supply is provided without delay."[56]

The power controversy received attention during Borden's Washington visit at the end of February, and the cooperative mood of the occasion seemed to make it amenable to solution. The Borden government, indeed, issued its command to supply the American firms only days later. But American officials indicated to Harris a month after that they still awaited results. In early April he wrote Borden:

> "You will realize the extreme awkwardness of the situation, as our whole talk when you were here and on all other occasions, has been along the line of Canada and the United States co-operating to the fullest possible extent, and the basis of our negotiations, and securing all the business possible for Canada, from the United States, always hinged more or less along this power situation. . . . that unless we can carry into action, what we have allowed the people here to believe we could do, I cannot see how we can consistently follow up our requests for the utilization of Canadian facilities.[57]

Clearly Harris had to be very sensitive to the wishes of U.S. officials with whom he spoke. Like representatives of any country in a foreign capital, moreover, Harris believed he understood the situation far better than his superiors at home. And the demands for coordination across the 49th parallel were indeed very real. As the *Canadian Annual Review* noted with regard to coal: "American fuel distributors in the Mining districts, American export licenses and control over coal movements, American exigencies of industrial and transport and terminal character, American "shutdowns" orders and embargoes and "coal-less days" had to be met or co-ordinated with Canadian conditions."[58] The whole thrust of Harris's effort was to meet these kinds of demands. He and his Mission tried to guide the continental movement of a North American economy under the impact of war. But while Harris and his War Mission represented the American viewpoint to Canadian policy-makers, their efforts were at all times centrally directed to insuring Canadian prosperity.

War demands, after all, required a formal coordination of the North American economy. To be sure, individual U.S. firms and industries had initiated a process of economic rationalization across the 49th parallel well before the turn of the century. The war, in this sense, simply accelerated an earlier trend. But Ottawa and Washington took increasing command of these relationships after 1914. They established through wartime administration what peacetime politics had made impossible.

The crisis made close, continuing Canadian representation in the American capital absolutely essential. Imperial organization could no longer fulfill this function, even though it made room for Canadian nationals, like C. B. Gordon. And traditional peacetime channels were ultimately closed as well. By the fall and winter of 1917-18, therefore, some kind of radical departure had become imperative, something which Lloyd Harris, for one, had recognized from personal experience in wartime Washington.

And so, the Canadian War Mission appeared, an organizational expression of the continental force of wartime economics. Paralleling this aspect of the Mission's function, its formation also registered the differentiation which occurred among British-Canadian relationships. The differences in perceptions and needs occasioned by the war required separate Canadian organization and representation for their expression. The emergence of the Canadian War Mission and Borden's pressure for representation at Versailles are simply different parts of the same process. The Great War forced a more systematic coordination of Canadian-American relations, even while it helped simultaneously to fragment the empire. It was a paradoxical effect which would emerge with even greater force during World War II.

CHAPTER FOUR

THE HYDE PARK DECLARATION,
1941: ORIGINS AND SIGNIFICANCE

"Done by Mackenzie and F.D.R. at Hyde Park on a grand Sunday, April 20, 1941." So Franklin Roosevelt inscribed the original typed copy of one of the most significant economic agreements reached between Canada and the United States during World War II. The simple six paragraph statement expressed the desire of President Roosevelt and Prime Minister Mackenzie King that "in mobilizing the resources of this continent each country should provide the other with the defense articles which it is best able to produce." The declaration anticipated that Canada "can supply the United States with between $200 million and $300 million worth of such defense articles" over the next year, purchases that would "materially assist Canada in meeting part of the cost of Canadian defense purchases in the United States." The agreement also specified that "In so far as Canadian defense purchases in the United States consist of component parts to be used in equipment and munitions which Canada is producing for Great Britain, it was also agreed that Great Britain will obtain these parts under the lease-lend act and forward them to Canada for inclusion in the finished articles."[1]

Mackenzie King regarded Hyde Park as a triumph of

personal diplomacy. When he spoke to the House of Commons about the declaration on April 28 he emphasized how it would reduce Canada's exchange problem with the United States and how it would contribute to the rationalization of continental defence production and so aid both Britain and the war effort. "But beyond its immediate significance," he continued, "the Hyde Park declaration will have a permanent significance in the relations between Canada and the United States. It involves nothing less than a common plan for the economic defence of the western hemisphere." More, the declaration was "a further convincing demonstration that Canada and the United States are indeed laying the enduring foundations of a new world order, an order based on international understanding, on mutual aid, on friendship and good will."[2]

Even if it did not live up to King's exuberant claims for it, the Hyde Park declaration was generally hailed in Canada by Liberals and Conservatives, by businessmen and farmers. It seemed to resolve some of Canada's pressing short-term problems and apparently without cost to the Dominion. But simple and straightforward as it was, the agreement still raises some important questions for the historian. Why was it necessary? What was the international context in which the agreement was signed?. How did Ottawa officials decide on the necessity for such an agreement? And how did Mackenzie King secure Roosevelt's cooperation?

These questions should help us reflect upon three broad historical issues of general importance. These are: first, Canada's place at this time in the so-called North Atlantic triangle; second, the general patterns of Canadian-American economic relations that began to emerge during the war years; and finally, the context of Canada's role in the emerging "new world order" of the post-war years.

These general themes should remind us of the obvious: Hyde Park did not occur in a vacuum. It was, rather, a consequence of Anglo-American financial diplomacy, and it followed in the wake of a series of prior agreements between the United States and the United Kingdom.

The Roosevelt Administration had made a number of breaches in the neutrality walls before 1941. But such measures as repeal of the arms embargo in 1939 and the destroyers-for-bases deal in 1940, though of importance to the Allies, had not solved Britain's growing shortage of gold and U.S. dollars. This was an issue that reached crisis proportions after the British assumed liability for French contracts in America with the fall of France in June, 1940. British purchases in North America, the Chancellor of the Exchequer estimated on 21 August, 1940, would run to $3.2 billion over the next year. But Britain's total resources in foreign exchange and American securities amounted at best to £490 million, and some of the securities virtually could not be sold.[3] The prospect was one of bankruptcy. "Boys," the British Ambassador, Lord Lothian, told the press on his return to the United States in late 1940, "Britain's broke. It's your money we want."[4]

The British plight, however, was not immediately perceived as such in Washington. Some key administration officials, especially in the State Department, repeatedly demonstrated scepticism about the extent of British financial hardship and a parallel belief in the opulence of empire. They advised British representatives to sell such direct investments in the United States as Shell Oil, Lever Brothers, and Brown and Williamson Tobacco in order to acquire both dollars and public good will.[5] They urged further that London seize gold supplies which Canada held in trust for the French, a proposal that would trouble Canada's relations with both Britain and the United States well into the next year.[6] President Roosevelt, who held an exaggerated view of British holdings, personally told Lothian in November, 1940 that Britain would have to liquidate $9 billion worth of assets in the Western hemisphere before she could expect to make a convincing case for aid.[7]

At this point, the Administration's request for liquidation owed less to a determination to break up the empire than to a concern to overcome isolationist opposition in Congress, to prove that the British were indeed in dire need. "Between 1939 and 1941," writes the latest student of Lend-Lease, "the formulation of American economic policy rested primarily with [Secretary of the Treasury Henry] Morgenthau and the Treasury Department, which thought essentially about restraining Nazism and pacifying public opinion."[8] The consequences for Britain and the Empire were serious nonetheless.

The Anglo-American financial difficulties that would eventually produce Lend-Lease had their parallel on a somewhat smaller scale in Anglo-Canadian relations, although sometimes the frictions were as great. There had been much irritation in London about Canada's unwillingness to assume more of a financial burden in the first few months of the war, particularly in connection with the British Commonwealth Air Training Plan,[9] but there had been equally sharp comments in Ottawa in 1939 and early 1940 about the British government's reluctance to place munitions orders in Canada.[10] Both British orders and British pressures increased following the fall of France, and feeling mounted in Whitehall that Canada should begin to use her own gold reserves and direct investments in the United States. Furthermore, British representatives, partly in response to American demands, continued to press Ottawa for the French gold.[11]

Spurred by the desperate war situation, the Canadian government soon took a series of steps to provide Britain with additional Canadian dollar supplies, among which the repatriation of Canadian securities held by British citizens was the most important. To 31 March, 1941, the British deficit with Canada was $795 million. Of this amount, 31.4 percent was met by gold transfers, 42.4 percent by debt repatriation, and 26.2 percent by the accumulation of sterling balances in London.[12] The British wanted Ottawa to contribute more by way of sterling overdrafts, in effect a form of dollar loan, in part to reduce the pace of redemption of Canadian securities. Moreover, by late 1940 the flow of British gold to Canada had come to a halt.

Britain's deteriorating financial position had serious implications for Canada. The historian of British war finance has pointed out that "Whether the Dominion Government provided the United Kingdom with Canadian dollars in exchange for repatriated Canadian securities or for a sterling balance, the dollars had to be found by the Dominion Government either by taxation or by the sale of securities to the Canadian public."[13] The problem for Canada was that the strain on the economy was already very great indeed. Estimates by Finance Minister J. L. Ilsley in February, 1941 were that war expenditures in fiscal 1941 would run to $1.4 billion while an additional $400 million would be needed for repatriation of securities from Britain and $433 million would be required for civil expenditures. In addition, Isley calculated, the municipal and provincial governments would spend $575 million. The total was $2.8 billion, well over half the national income.[14] If the British financial position deteriorated further, the demands on Canada would increase, and the result might be, as Mackenzie King gloomily ruminated, "a greater burden than the people of Canada can be led to bear."[15] A solution to British financial problems was an absolute necessity for Canada.

Even under peacetime conditions Canada's economy

was based on a "bilateral unbalance within a balanced 'North Atlantic Triangle'."[16] Canada had a chronic deficit with the United States, in other words, but it had been balanced — and generally more than balanced — by a surplus with Britain, Western Europe, and empire countries. Much of that market had disappeared as a result of the war, of course, and Britain was now financially strapped. In the meantime, trade had increased with the United States, most of it as a direct result of the war. In April, 1941, the Deputy Minister of Finance foresaw a deficit of $478 million in Canada's balance of payments with the U.S., and by June, Canadian officials estimated that American imports had increased by $400 million per year over the 1938 figures while Canadian exports to the United States had risen by only half as much.[17] So long as thirty percent of the components required for British munitions orders had to be secured by Canada from the United States, there was little prospect of a reduction in the deficit. The result, in sum, was that Canada faced the problem of having to finance Britain's deficit while itself facing an increasing deficit of American dollars. The double bind was tightening.

The King government took a series of actions in its efforts to right this adverse balance with the United States after Canada entered the war. A Foreign Exchange Control Order to prevent capital exports was issued in 1939, and it was accompanied by increased efforts to broaden exports, stimulate American tourism in Canada, and to increase gold production. Further measures followed in the spring and fall of 1940, including the stabilization of the exchange rate at ten percent below parity with the American dollar and a refusal of American dollar exchange for Canadian travellers to the United States. In December, 1940, the government took its most serious step in a move that coincided with the end of British gold flows to

Canada. The passage of the War Exchange Conservation Act prohibited importation of a long list of products (including cereals, processed and canned fruits and vegetables, spirits and wines, electric appliances and jewelry) from countries outside the sterling bloc.[18] Clearly the measure was aimed at reducing imports from the United States. Simultaneously the government lowered duties on a large number of imports from Britain and levied heavy excise taxes on automobiles and other articles which required large imports of American components.[19] These measures were expected to save $70 million in exchange.[20] But the adverse trade balance continued its inexorable increase.[21]

Equally as important as the devices the government used to cope with the exchange problem are the options it rejected. In late October, 1940, for instance, the very able U.S. Minister in Ottawa, Pierrepont Moffat, had informed Washington that "Canada's biggest worry at the moment is financial — how to acquire more dollar exchange." "The need," Moffat said,

> is not yet desperate but the problem is rapidly becoming acute. It could, of course, be staved off if our legislation were amended and loans or credits granted to Canada, but there is some slight opposition to this prospect in financial circles here which argue that the future headache of servicing a large increase in Canada's foreign debt would be worse than any possible current headache. If loans or credits are not soon forthcoming then we must face the fact that Canada will have to take one or more of the following three measures: (A) Seizure against compensation and sale in New York of large blocks of American securities now held by Canadians; (B) Blocking in whole or in part the transfer to American owners of dividends from American companies; and (C) Selective purchasing from the United States under license, with strict rationing of non-essentials, among which are included American fruits and vegetables. There is much popular pressure in favour of number three.[22]

The reaction in financial circles in the United States to any move to block dividends flowing out of Canada would have been very sharp, of course. The War Exchange Conservation Act, then, was extremely significant for what it omitted.

At the same time, however, several points that would become issues in subsequent Canadian-American negotiations appeared in early strategy discussions. Clearly Ottawa officials wanted to avoid borrowing in the United States. Moffat had reported opposition to the idea in October, and O. D. Skelton, the Under Secretary of State for External Affairs, had observed that Ilsley believed "it would be disastrous to face a future of making heavy interest payments to the United States year after year in perpetuity, or, alternatively, having a war debt controversy."[23] On this point, in fact, Canadian and American policy converged, for one of the central objects of Lend-Lease would be to avoid just this kind of postwar entanglement with the British.

A second point to emerge, and one which would remain central to Canadian policy in the subsequent months, was Canada's determination to hold on to her investments in the United States. Estimates of the amount in question varied from $275 million to over $1 billion,[24] and while Finance Department officers were prepared to consider a sell-off *in extremis*, they clearly hoped to avoid such an unpalatable measure. The Canadian investments provided a cushion that protected Canada from some of the strains imposed by the nation's heavy foreign indebtedness and, among a host of additional economic reasons, there was the real difficulty involved in compelling Canadians to sell their holdings in American securities at what some investors would feel to be sacrifice prices.[25] Both the British and the Americans would challenge Ottawa's position, but without success.

Finally, King and his officials took a very cautious approach to putting controls on United States imports, and with good reason. Such controls flew in the face of the prewar trend toward liberalized trade between the two countries and would be certain to antagonize U.S. Secretary of State Cordell Hull, one of Canada's champions in the American capital. They would also invite powerful opposition from American domestic interests, and this could block amicable agreements in other, more crucial policy areas. This kind of calculation almost certainly entered the decision to omit fresh fruits and vegetables from the December list of excluded imports. As Ilsley frankly told Parliament, "we had to weigh . . . the inevitable public reaction there would be in many of the agricultural districts of the United States, the embarrassment this restriction would cause . . . and the danger which would ensue not only to our own trade relations with the United States, not only to the market which our trade agreement with that country gives to so many of our primary producers, but to the whole trade agreement policy of the United States."[26]

As 1940 gave way to the new year both Canadian and British calculations centered increasingly upon the proposed Lend-Lease Act. Introduced by Roosevelt into Congress on January 10, the bill was designed to speed up munitions production, to eliminate the need for cash payments on Allied orders, and to increase Roosevelt's freedom in foreign affairs. It empowered the President to have manufactured "any defense article for the government of any country whose defense the President deems vital to the defense of the United States." These articles he could "sell, transfer title to, exchange, lend, lease, or otherwise dispose of" to those governments.[27]

For the next three months officials in London and Ottawa waited upon Congress to accept this dramatic shift in the ground rules of U.S. aid. But British and Canadian calculations diverged in at least two important respects. For London, the introduction of Lend-Lease would end the first stage of negotiation with the United States and open wider the doorway to America's productive and financial might. For Ottawa, however, the passage of the Lend-Lease Act would mean not only that the first stage of negotiations was about to begin but that Britain might close the door to future orders in Canada. Canadian enthusiasm for any Lend-Lease aid to the war effort, therefore, coexisted with anxiety over the future of Anglo-Canadian relations.

What would happen to British orders placed in Canada once Lend-Lease became law? This was a key question for Canadian officials. C. D. Howe, the Minister of Munitions and Supply, told his Cabinet War Committee colleagues on February 18 that he was "gravely concerned" that the American legislation might lead the British to shift orders for raw materials, food and munitions to the United States where the terms seemed easier.[28] Some ten days later Howe was pressing for the despatch of a strong negotiating team to Washington to talk with both American and British officials, and he was warning his colleagues that the diversion of orders could have "disastrous" results on the country's industrial programme.[29]

That the British fully appreciated the impact Lend-Lease would have on Anglo-Canadian relations seems certain. Some lesser ministers bemoaned what they saw as Canada's accelerating drift out of the empire and into the American orbit,[30] but the Treasury, however, clearly wanted Canada to use Lend-Lease to the fullest. This was crystal clear in a Treasury brief prepared for the newly named High Commissioner to Canada, Malcolm MacDonald:

What we want Canada to do, is (a) to reduce her purchases in the United States to an absolute minimum. . . . (b) To make use herself of the "Lease and Lend" Bill if the United States Government will agree to this, in order to obtain the maximum she can from the United States without payment. (c) In so far as Canada still has an adverse balance with the United States ... to cover this with saleable Canadian marketable assets (e.g. United States securities, etc.) held by Canada.

This prescription was recognized as being difficult for the Canadians to swallow. They would need heavier taxation, the Treasury brief noted, and they would have to accept some inflation. "But clearly their objective should be to meet our needs so far as possible by saving and taxation and to reduce inflation to a minimum." The brief concluded by noting that the British held a good hand in negotiating with Canada.

These are points of domestic policy on which we have no right to dictate to Canada, but it is as much in their interests as in ours to act along these lines, seeing that our only alternative, if we are unable to pay for our orders in Canada, is to place them instead in the United States in cases in which we should be able to obtain the goods under the "lease and lend" Act.[31]

This Treasury position was consistent with the British line throughout the war thus far: Canada could do more. But the British now possessed a powerful weapon in Lend-Lease, and access to the $7 billion Congressional appropriation which accompanied it greatly increased their manoeuverability. Unless and until Canada could reach a settlement with the British on purchasing policy, Lend-Lease would increase the unpredictability of Anglo-Canadian financial relations.

And what of Canada's relationship with the United States under Lend-Lease? Opinion was developing among top officers in the Finance Department that Canada should have none of it. The British Treasury's representative in North America noted that Clifford Clark, the Deputy Minister of Finance, was opposed, despite his country's adverse balance with the United States and steeply mounting loans to Britain. Clark believed that acceptance would place Canada in a weaker position vis-à-vis the United States than Britain, separated by an ocean from American power, and that the Americans later might drive a very hard bargain on tariffs.[32] The Prime Minister accepted this reasoning, too. As he wrote in his diary on March 13,

> We do not intend to avail ourselves of the Lend-Lease Bill but to allow its advances wholly to Britain. There is, of course, a bigger obligation because of it all than appears on the face of it. I have no doubt the U.S. would undoubtedly keep the obligations arising under the Lend-Lease Bill hanging pretty much over her head to be used to compel open markets or return of materials etc. It is a terrible position for Britain to be in.[33]

As we have seen, one of the assumptions of the Ottawa planners that led to their hesitancy about Lend-Lease was their fear that Washington would demand a liquidation of Canadian assets in the United States similar to that pressed upon Britain. They were also aware that some Americans believed that Canada had not done as much as she could to aid Britain. There was, for example, the matter of French gold that Canada was holding in trust for France and refusing to turn over to the British, and there were also complaints that Canada was charging the British for all her purchases while the United States was being expected to give Britain supplies for free under Lend-Lease.[34] Treasury Secretary Morgenthau personally told Clifford Clark at an early stage in the Canadian-American conversations that Canada would not be permitted to come under Lend-Lease unless "steps had been taken to realize at least a portion of

Canadian securities in the United States." Nor was Morgenthau particularly worried that any rapid Canadian liquidation would further depress stock market prices, already reacting to the British sale of the Viscose Corporation.[35]

What Canada clearly was seeking was some way to have whatever benefits were available under Lend-Lease to solve her exchange problems, while avoiding the kinds of sacrifices demanded of the British both in the short-run (liquidation of direct investments) and in the long-run (weakened bargaining position in the post-war years). The problem was to hit on a formula that obviated direct Lend-Lease aid, that did not add to Morgenthau's problems with Congress, and yet still reduced Canada's call on U.S. dollars. The ideal situation from Canada's point of view would be an arrangement whereby Washington agreed to buy some of its war needs in Canada and also to supply the components Canada required for manufacturing munitions for the British. And if, in addition, Washington could be persuaded to buy Canadian output for shipment to England under Lend-Lease, Ottawa would have access to British purchasing while avoiding the current requirement of financing it.

The War Committee heard one part of this formula on March 12. The Deputy Minister of Finance had seen Morgenthau and suggested that the raw materials and components Canada required to manufacture munitions for Britain should be eligible for Lend-Lease on the British account.[36] Grant Dexter, the ubiquitous *Winnipeg Free Press* reporter, met with T. A. Crerar, the Minister of Mines and Resources, on the 25th, and similarly learned that the government was "trying to persuade the U.S. to include in the Lease and Lend category, the raw materials shipped to Canada for manufacture and re-shipment to [Britain]." That would give some relief on balance of payments. The problem was that "Washington, [Crerar] said, is pretty sticky with Canada so far as Lease and Lend goes."[37]

Washington indeed was being sticky. Morgenthau, feeling bound by his pledges to Congress, was not very helpful when Canadian and British financial officials saw him on March 18 and 19. If there were exchange problems, Canada should begin to liquidate her securities, he said, and as for the question of bringing the British component of Canadian imports from the United States under Lend-Lease, that was for Harry Hopkins to decide.[38] Hopkins was Roosevelt's friend and confidant and the man charged by the President with the administration of Lend-Lease. As a result, Clifford Clark was convinced by the end of March that Morgenthau was the chief obstacle to a favourable settlement,[39] and he was increasingly of the view, as he told Grant Dexter on April 9, that "a good deal of education was needed in the U.S. to prove to them that it was not in their own interest to put Canada through the wringer."[40] This task of education would ultimately fall to Mackenzie King.

In the meantime, the British had agreed to maintain their orders in Canada. Word had reached Ottawa in mid-March that the British would not divert orders from Canada if the Canadians would agree to assume financial responsibility for them.[41] This was something close to blackmail, even if the British no longer had any alternative to such a course, and the Canadian government had to go along. By March 27 Finance Minister Ilsley had drafted a telegram agreeing to finance British orders placed in Canada.[42] To this extent, the British had used Lend-Lease to bargain very effectively and toughly with Ottawa. But this agreement with London may have served to strengthen Canada's hand with Washington. It further justified the Canadian request for an arrangement to ease the exchange problem, and it also visibly demonstrated an intensification of Canada's financial war effort.

Congress passed Lend-Lease on March 11, and the time to settle with Washington had now arrived. At the Cabinet War Committee on March 21, Ilsley said that his deputy minister, Clifford Clark, was convinced that only direct representations to President Roosevelt could produce immediate and sympathetic consideration of Canada's difficulties in retaining and financing British purchases in Canada. At this meeting, the Prime Minister indicated that he was planning a trip to Washington in April.[43] It now would be up to King personally to secure a favourable agreement from the Roosevelt Administration.

Negotiation was the kind of task at which Mackenzie King excelled. He was a shrewd judge of men, and he was as confident in his own prowess as a negotiator as was President Roosevelt. Both leaders believed that their charm, when applied full force, was an effective weapon. And both men, after a series of meetings since 1935, knew each other fairly well. To Roosevelt, King was "Mackenzie" and a skillful, long-lived politician. To King, Roosevelt was still "Mr. President" but there was a good deal of genuine admiration in this relationship. Archibald MacLeish, the poet and head of the Library of Congress, saw King in February, 1941, and wrote to the President of his host's parting words: "he asked me if I would remember him to you and then turned and came back and said, with a sudden and very real warmth: 'Give him my love.' I have never heard words spoken with more sincerity."[44] Though one can scarcely conceive of similar words being seriously spoken by Roosevelt, the President, as L.B. Pearson noted, "had a better understanding of the position and importance of Canada than most Americans in official places."[45] That was probably more important than mere sentiment. Mackenzie King, too, had a genuine understanding of the United States and its political problems. He had, for example, deliberately refrained from saying anything whatsoever about Lend-Lease during the long debate about it in the Congress. More, he had taken no steps to explain the Canadian war effort to the United States during the last several months.[46] This was conscious and deliberate policy, for by keeping a low profile for Canada he kept the Dominion from impinging on the American consciousness as yet another nation seeking a handout. He may even have hoped to ease Roosevelt's difficulties with Congress by his silence, for the isolationist America Firsters eagerly seized on bellicose foreign speeches and used them as evidence of interference.

King left for Washington on April 15 and saw the President the next day. Their first conversation was mainly about hemispheric military matters, the subject that clearly was uppermost in Roosevelt's mind. The United States was going to extend its patrols further out into the Atlantic, he said, and the President demonstrated that he was well briefed about the defence of the Labrador coast. Mackenzie King "purposely refrained from discussing financial matters," he recorded in his diary, "as I saw how tired he was, and did not wish to introduce this subject until we got away when we could discuss it quietly."[47]

The next day King saw Secretary of State Hull and Treasury Secretary Morgenthau in separate appointments. Hull was friendly and the two men chatted politely about a wide range of subjects. King soon got down to business, however, and told Hull that he hoped it would be possible to have "the components of materials we were producing for Britain secured from America on the Lend-Lease American basis and that America would place orders with us for things that we could produce."[48] The reciprocal nature of the proposed arrangement was clear, a shrewd tactic on King's part for reciprocity was a sacred totem of international relations to Hull. Ironically, however, Hull was extremely lukewarm about Lend-Lease, and the great aid bill had been pressed for mainly by Morgenthau.[49]

The Treasury Secretary was in an expansive mood but he stressed his difficulties with Congress and told King that in order to get Lend-Lease passed he had had to make clear that Britain was bankrupt. As far as Morgenthau was concerned, Canada was not yet in that state. King recorded that the Secretary "thought our situation was all right till the end of the year," and the Prime Minister had to stress to Morgenthau that Canada in fact was in great difficulties at that moment. King then raised his idea for a virtual system of barter in war materials between Canada and the United States and found Morgenthau interested and willing to do "anything possible . . . on this scale to help to get us purchasing power." The Secretary also said "they would pay in dollars for things manufactured by us. I said it would go to purchasing American war material." The two agreed that Clifford Clark would meet the Secretary the next day to discuss matters further.[50]

Matters seemed to be in hand at last. And on Sunday, April 20, just before he was to go to Hyde Park, Roosevelt's home on the Hudson River, King met with Clark and E. P. Taylor of Munitions and Supply. The Deputy Minister of Finance gave King a draft statement that expressed the optimum state of affairs from the Canadian point of view. Mackenzie King, after making a few amendments, carried this draft with him when he went off to spend his "grand Sunday" with the President.[51]

It was indeed to be a grand Sunday, particularly for Canada and Mackenzie King. The visit was long and friendly, and Roosevelt again talked at length about hemisphere defence, aid to Britain, and American bases in Canada and Newfoundland. Later in the afternoon, Roosevelt said that he had seen Morgenthau and had the Canadian situation explained to him. "He thought perhaps it might be going a little too far to have something manufactured in Canada for the U.S. to Lease-Lend to England,"[52] King recorded.

After a pleasant dinner, the discussion turned in earnest to the subject King had come to discuss. The Prime Minister produced his draft agreement and showed it to the President who "Said he thought it was first rate." There were only two changes requested by the President. As he had indicated earlier in the afternoon to King, he deleted any reference to the United States purchasing goods in Canada for subsequent Lend-Lease to Britain. The President also added aluminum to a list of war materials Canada could supply to the United States. The amended Canadian draft was agreed to over the telephone by Morgenthau, and the Hyde Park Agreement was fact. It had all been incredibly easy.[53]

King was justifiably proud of his success, and he was heaped with praise by his Cabinet colleagues. C. D. Howe, in particular, his munitions plants now virtually assured of continuous full production, was glowing. "Said something about being the greatest negotiator the country had or something about the world's best negotiator," King wrote in his Record. "Could hardly believe so much could have been accomplished in so short a time. Said it straightened out the most difficult problems they had had for months."[54] So it did. But what is most significant is that King secured his agreement without being forced to make any major concessions. After all the long and frustrating negotiations Clifford Clark and his colleagues had had with their American counterparts, nothing in the end was demanded of Canada.[55]

Once the agreement was signed, the rest was housekeeping. As early as April 24, the United States Army began to honour the agreement even before the modalities were clarified.[56] The details were not arranged until May 14, when Clifford Clark and Sir Frederick Phillips of the British Treasury signed a brief memornadum in Washington that put on record Britain's willingness to secure approximately $220 million worth of goods under Lend-Lease for despatch to Canada. This would represent "the actual value of the 'United States content' of Canadian war supplies to the United Kingdom."[57] Morgenthau accepted this arrangement, and the remaining details were worked out in a similar fashion.[58]

The Hyde Park Declaration, of course, did not solve all of Canada's manufacturing and exchange problems. There were continuing difficulties in maintaining British purchases in Canada that lasted until Canada adopted its Mutual Aid programme in early 1943.[59] As the agreement worked out in practice, moreover, the positive effects for Canada owed less to the provision of components intended for Britain under Lend-Lease than to increased American purchases in Canada. These mounted very fast, reaching $200 million by mid-1941, and totalling $275 million in 1942, $301 million in 1943, and $314 million in 1944.[60] Additional U.S. dollars soon flowed into Canada when the United States began heavy defence expenditures in the Canadian North West after Pearl Harbor, and when American investors, speculating on a revaluation of the undervalued Canadian dollar, began sending large sums north of the border. The result was that Canada's shortage of U.S. dollars was over by 1942 and the holdings, in fact, grew large enough the following year that controls had to be imposed to keep them within bounds.[61]

Ironically, therefore, many of the benefits for which King negotiated so successfully at Hyde Park would probably have accrued to Canada in any case after Pearl Harbor. The increased United States orders for defence materials, for example, would probably have been placed as soon as the Americans entered the war. The long-term economic significance of the agreement, then, was not great except insofar as it foretold the integration of the North American economies that we live with today. But Hyde Park was important, primarily for the way in which it was negotiated.

The origins of the declaration provide an insight into the broader historical patterns of these years. First of all, it is clear that Hyde Park emerged as a consequence of a bilateral arrangement between the United States and Britain. It is true that the Canadians were aware of the discussions that led up to the introduction of Lend-Lease into Congress in January, 1941. But apparently at no time were they included in these negotiations. Nor did British and American officials have Canada very much in mind as they established the Lend-Lease framework, except to hope that Ottawa would release the French gold to ease Britain's U.S. debt. The British, moreover, did not make any prior arrangements as to the source of their North American purchases, and this in turn caused grave apprehension among Canadian planners. For the most part, then, Canadian officials had to manoeuvre within economic boundaries staked out by the Americans and the British for their own purposes and goals. But this fact in itself was not necessarily detrimental to the Canadian position, nor did it make any subsequent action a foregone conclusion. On the contrary, Canada received several significant benefits from the prior Anglo-American negotiations, not the least of which was the opportunity for an agreement like Hyde Park.

Well before Mackenzie King set off for Washington in April, Canadian business circles, for example, realized the several opportunities which passage of Lend-Lease legislation would open up to Ottawa. Kenneth Wilson of *The Financial Post* had outlined them in a prescient article as early as 1 February, 1941, in which he noted that

Lend-Lease could lessen the need for import controls and exchange restrictions against the United States. The act offered three alternatives in this respect: the United States could ease Canadian dollar commitments by providing certain defence items; the United States could agree to buy certain materials from Canada and thus provide a supply of dollar exchange; and finally the Americans might finance branch-plant expansion in Canada for munitions production, buy the output and then send it to England through Lend-Lease.[62] This last, of course, was the most multipurpose proposal of all. In the end Mackenzie King pressed for a variation of all three alternatives and counted himself a lucky man to come away from Hyde Park with even the first two.

But why was King able to leave Hyde Park that Sunday in April with anything at all? And why without reciprocal concessions? Roosevelt did not demand that Canada turn over to the British (and hence ultimately to the United States) the French gold held in trust in Ottawa. He did not force the sale of Canada's American securities, nor did he demand withdrawal of the various Canadian measures designed to conserve exchange. The answers to these questions illustrate both general features of Canadian–American relations during the war years as well as the unique importance of the cordial relationship between the Prime Minister and the President.

In its broadest perspective, the agreement at Hyde Park did not matter much to the United States, even though there was an American preoccupation with hemispheric defence through 1940 and 1941. The very absence of any mention of the agreement in the memoirs of the major members of the Roosevelt Administration instrumental in working out Lend-Lease and the details of Anglo-American finance attests to this fact. The financial costs of Hyde Park were very small to the United States as well, particularly when they were compared with the $7 billion appropriation devoted to Lend-Lease. Nor did the agreement require a separate appropriation which would have singled out Canada for Congressional scrutiny. At the same time, however, it should be noted that the United States would secure access to Canadian war material of kinds and types it required. So obviously there was some benefit for Washington in the agreement.

Still, it was the United States that was offering the favour and Canada that was gratefully accepting it. Part of the reason for the Americans' willingness to help Canada must simply have been the genuine goodwill that existed between the two leaders, governments and peoples. Two Canadians who spent much of the war working in Washington for the Canadian government tried to explain this goodwill in an essay in 1945. They stressed that Canada's natural resources were vitally important to the United States, that the Canadian war effort was a highly creditable one, and that Ottawa was physically so close to Washington. "We could always bring a man to Washington to talk to his opposite number and since they spoke the same language and had the same approach to problems the results were generally satisfactory." Moreover Canada was a cash customer of the United States and was not seeking a handout. "In short," they say, "the United States trusted us, liked us, understood us, had no reason to fear us, and shared with us the common objective of defeating the enemy."[63] This is close to being a classic formulation of the "good neighbourhood" theory of continental relations, but some of it may be true for all that.

More realistically, another harder factor that must be mentioned is that by the beginning of the Second World War, the United States had an investment in Canada of $4.15 billion and this amounted to fully sixty percent of the total foreign investment in Canada.[64] For the United

States to squeeze Canada involved squeezing its subsidiaries as well, and too vigorous action might have forced Ottawa to take action against the branch-plants and their shareholders in the United States.

Above all, however, was the willingness of President Roosevelt to receive Mackenzie King and to listen to him. Had the issue not reached Roosevelt there is no certainty that the result would have been so favourable to Canadian interests. Of course, Roosevelt was committed heart and soul to the defeat of the Axis, and he was willing to go just as far as he could to aid Britain and the Allies. But his primary concern was with military and strategic questions, and he was far, far less interested in economic matters that he may not have entirely understood in any case.

Mackenzie King was clearly aware of this and he pitched his appeal to Roosevelt in terms that were precisely calculated. In an interview with Grant Dexter the day after the agreement was signed, King revealed the approach he had employed:

> ... Roosevelt had said to King that he didn't know much about the exchange situation: that he would like King to tell him about it and outline the policy which Roosevelt should follow. King hadn't bothered about the economics of it. He told Roosevelt that if he were in his place, he would have regarded [sic] only for the neighbourly phase of it. What the U.S. and Britain had done was one thing. Canada as the neighbour on this continent, the only one that really mattered, was another proposition entirely. If the U.S. insisted upon taking from Canada what few possessions she had in the U.S. it would only give voice to anti-U.S. sentiment in this country. Why not buy from Canada as much as Canada is buying from the U.S. — just balance the accounts. Roosevelt thought this was a swell idea.[65]

Roosevelt was much better briefed than this account suggests, and certainly he was not the passive figure King paints him as here. But the Dexter memorandum catches perfectly the style and tone of an appeal that was calculated to work with Roosevelt far better than statistics, charts, and financial data. The Prime Minister knew how to court a king.

For Mackenzie King the lesson of Hyde Park was that Canada and the United States were "laying the enduring foundations of a new world order."[66] A new world order was being created and there can be no doubt of that. Britain was being reduced to the status of a lesser power and the United States was reaching the super-power status she still occupies. But for King to suggest as he did that Canada was shaping this new order with Washington was wishful thinking. It would have been more to the point for King to say that Canada was working to achieve such benefits as it could under the new American order. The Hyde Park agreement may indicate that Canada could do this much with some success in 1941.

CHAPTER FIVE

GETTING ON WITH THE AMERICANS: CANADIAN PERCEPTIONS OF THE UNITED STATES, 1939-1945

The Hyde Park Agreement illustrated as well as any international agreement could the joining of economic considerations with emotional considerations. The economic problems could readily be solved if there was a will to do so. But the emotional links between Canada and its vastly more powerful neighbour posed special problems that would persist, particularly as the war proceeded and forced the two countries into greater interdependency. Despite this, the Second World War is regularly trumpeted as the period in which Canada came of age. The nation contributed very substantially to the Allied victory in men, material, and foodstuffs, and as a result of this effort Canada emerged from the war as perhaps the leader of a group of middle powers. There was a very great distance between a middle and a great power, to be sure, but there can be no doubt that fortunate geographical circumstance and economic power had combined to give Canada a status far beyond anything she had enjoyed before.

But in a sense this was artificial. During the war, as Professor C. P. Stacey has effectively demonstrated in his magisterial study of Canadian war policies, Canada was essentially unsuccessful in getting much of a share in Allied decision-making.[1] Power was concentrated in the hands of the "Big Three" and there was no disposition to share it, no matter how valuable the contribution of Canada and other lesser states might be.

This was no less true of the United States than of the Soviet Union or Great Britain, and this came as something of a shock to Canadian statesmen. Relations with the Americans had been increasingly warm after 1935, and Prime Minister Mackenzie King for a time was fully convinced that his destiny was to serve as the linch-pin that would link Great Britain and her estranged former colony. With their heavy capital investment in Canada and a growing trade surplus to protect, American leaders reciprocated Mackenzie King's friendship, and a special relationship seemed firmly established. The outbreak of war made this a valuable asset to Canada and to Britain, and King was exceedingly successful in the way he exploited his position in the period before Pearl Harbour.

Perhaps he was too successful, for the war linked the two North American states into economic lockstep, while the military exigencies led to a large American presence in Canada. This state of affairs might have been marginally acceptable to Canada if there had been an accretion of influence in Washington to offset it, but if such an intangible as influence can be measured, after mid-1941 there was probably an absolute decline. The effects were serious to Canada, and they preoccupied planners more and more as the war progressed and planning for the peace began.

The requirements of defence had begun to force closer cooperation on Canada and the United States even before 1939. A first meeting between military staff officers of both countries, arranged in secret and with the direct authorization of President Franklin Roosevelt and Prime Minister King, took place in January, 1938 and a second meeting followed eleven months later.[2] More important, since offered in a public statement, was Roosevelt's pledge in a speech at Queen's University in Kingston, Ontario in August, 1938: "The Dominion of Canada is part of the sisterhood of the British Empire. I give to you assurance that the people of the United States will not stand idly by if domination of Canadian soil is threatened by any other Empire."[3] "What I said at Queen's University," Roosevelt wrote in a private letter to Lord Tweedsmuir, the Governor General of Canada, "was so obvious that I cannot quite understand why some American President did not say it half a century ago."[4]

The importance of the American pledge became evident after September, 1939. The war was supposed to be one of "limited liability" for Canada, one that could be won without huge expenditures of men or money. The British and French shared similar views, too, and the Allied leaders and press talked optimistically of the blockade that would force Germany to its knees. The dreams of easy victory, however, dissolved into the reality of May and June, 1940. Suddenly Britain found herself in danger of invasion and bereft of her French ally. For Canada, the character of the war altered overnight, and the Dominion all at once became England's ranking ally. The prospect of a British defeat was real, and in the circumstances Canadians cautiously began to look to their own safety.

The United States was Canada's only salvation. This was clear. Fortunately, there had been no major gaffes to alienate the Roosevelt administration or the American public. War measures that would affect the United States, its citizens or its corporations had been canvassed fully in Washington before implementation.[5] And with a few exceptions Canadians managed to restrain themselves while the isolationists and interventionists hammered away at one another in the United States.[6]

The deliberate and cautious low profile maintained by Canada in the first months of the war was probably appreciated in Washington. As a result Canada was in a good position to deal with the United States in this time of troubles. The first task was to play the role of middleman between London and Washington. King had hoped for this earlier, but now in the very different circumstances of spring, 1940 he found this chore very difficult and taxing indeed.

The future of the Royal Navy in the event of a British defeat was obviously of great importance to Roosevelt. With the fleet in its hands, Germany could be a direct threat to America. Without it, or with the fleet in the American service, there would be no practical risks at all. The problem was that some Empire statesmen, most notably Menzies of Australia, saw the fleet as a bargaining counter that could induce the United States to give aid to the foundering Allies. An appeal cast in those terms clearly offended Roosevelt, who told a Canadian emissary that the message seemed to say "If you don't help us at once we will let the Germans have the Fleet and you can go to Hell."[7] But what would happen to the Royal Navy "in the event of certain possible eventualities which could not possibly be mentioned aloud"?[8]

Roosevelt wanted Mackenzie King to convey to Prime Minister Winston Churchill the American hope that the Royal Navy would be preserved if the worst came to pass. In the event of a surrender, the President told H. L. Keenleyside, the External Affairs officer who served as King's emissary, the fleet should be dispersed to the Empire and the royal family despatched to Ottawa, perhaps, or to some other safe location. By that time, American opinion would be ready to help the Allies. But if Hitler took the Royal Navy, the result would be disaster. Japan would gain a virtually free hand in the Pacific and the empire would be divided between Germany and Italy. Then came the difficult part for Mackenzie King. Keenleyside told the Prime Minister that the President wanted him to persuade the other Dominions to make a joint appeal to Churchill not to surrender the fleet.

King was appalled since such a request could only imply a lack of faith in Churchill's determination. As he recorded in his diary, "for a moment it seemed to me that the United States was seeking to save itself at the expense of Britain. That it was an appeal to the selfishness of the Dominions at the expense of the British Isles. ... I instinctively revolted against such a thought. My reaction was that I would rather die than do aught to save ourselves or any part of this continent at the expense of Britain." The worst was yet to come. After he sent Keenleyside back to see Roosevelt to clarify the point, King learned that he was expected to present the President's view as if it were his own. The result was that King spent a very difficult May 30th trying to draft a message so as to "meet the President's wishes ... of having the message appear to be from myself rather than from him, while at the same time taking care to see that it was wholly his point of view that I was putting over and not my own."[9] The middleman's role was not an easy one, and Churchill's understandable irritation showed through his answering despatches. "Although the President is our best friend," he telegraphed to King, "no practical help has yet been forthcoming from the United States,"[10] a hard but true statement.

For Mackenzie King this period was an agonizing one. His world was crumbling, and he was near despair. Grant Dexter, the reporter for the *Winnipeg Free Press*, with the best contacts in Ottawa, saw J. L. Ralston, King's Minister of Finance, on June 7th and was told of the Prime Minister's condition:

Ralston had found King in his office at 2 a.m. working on this proposition [one of the liaison roles he was filling between Churchill and Roosevelt]. King had said that he was played out, finished and couldn't carry the load, or words to this effect. Ralston told me he said: "Chief you've got to go through. The despatch you are working on may mean victory, the saving of civilization." King agreed.[11]

Of equal importance, particularly from the Canadian point of view, was the formal defence tie that was made with the United States in the summer of 1940. The idea was not a new one, but before the fall of France few would have believed it either necessary or expedient. Mr. Justice Felix Frankfurter, a close confidant of the President, told the Canadian Minister in Washington in early July that a common defence scheme was necessary.[13] Similarly a group of influential Canadians, mainly academics, younger politicians and lawyers associated through the Canadian Institute of International Affairs, had drawn up a "Program of Immediate Canadian Action" at a meeting in July. Their concerns were fixed on the potential economic difficulties Canada faced with much of Europe now closed to her trade, but even more they argued the need for "conversations with the United States aiming at a continental defence scheme. . . . Public opinion in Canada," they claimed, "is ready for a frank recognition by the government of the need for action." Time was of the essence and Canada had to take the initiative. "If Canada allows this opportunity to go by default and the United States is consequently [later] obliged to require us to cooperate, we might as a result be unable to maintain our independent identity."[14]

Economic issues also concerned official Ottawa. The Bank of Canada had set up a committee in June to explore what steps would be necessary if, as it was euphemistically stated, communications with the United Kingdom were cut. The results, the subsequent study argued, would be catastrophic, and there would be heavy unemployment as industries lost their overseas markets. Canada would have to appeal to the United States for assistance, Graham Towers of the Bank wrote to King, and almost the only card that Canada held was that "The United States will have to plan its defence on continental terms at least, and Canada will be an integral and necessary part of their plan."[15]

Certainly the Americans knew this, for their exports to Europe and Britain were in much the same position as Canada's. The result was a sharp turn toward hemispheric thinking in Washington. Bruce Hutchison, the reporter for the Sifton newspapers, visited Washington early in June and had an astonishing conversation with A. A. Berle, the theorist of the large-scale corporation who had served in Roosevelt's brains trust. By 1940, Berle was an Assistant Secretary of State and, as Hutchison put it a bit too fulsomely, "the President's very closest adviser and brain man." Berle's studies, the reporter noted in a memorandum that found its way to Mackenzie King, "now relate to the new American Empire. I can describe it as nothing else. He has been working, he said, on the re-organization of the economy of all North and South America, the new hemispheric concept." Where, Hutchison asked, did Canada fit in all this?

> Well, [Berle said] it's a problem, but not as great as you might think. Don't forget that we are going in for huge armaments. This will provide a large employment for Canadians. Then there are such factors as the end of Scandinavian paper exports. You will get this business in the U.S. Wheat is the headache. But there, too, we will have to make concessions. You people still talk Manchester Liberalism. All right, we'll apply it to wheat. We'll say to the wheat producers, we can take so much wheat at a fixed price guaranteed by the government. You can produce more than that if you please,

but you'll take whatever price the market will pay. In the end, your wheat men will get less and many of them will move into other industries. That has to come with us and with you, too. It was coming anyway. My feeling, in fact, is that the war has made it possible to settle many such problems, including the future of trade between the U.S. and Canada, which we could not settle in peace time. In these times Congress will be willing to do many things it would never do before.

"His whole assumption," Hutchison concluded, "was that Canada's economy would be merged with that of the U.S., but he did not foresee political union."[16] Berle's scheme seemed predicated on a British defeat, of course.

Canadians could not publicly concede a British defeat as a possibility, although the Bank of Canada study indicated that planning for such an eventuality was in hand. H. L. Keenleyside wanted something more. "It is no longer any secret," Keenleyside wrote, "that the Government of the United States has been giving detailed and serious consideration to the possibility of reorganizing the whole economic life of the Western Hemisphere." Canadians had not studied this question at all, he argued, nor had they given much thought to the "military necessity for a revision of our external policies":

It would seem to be improbable that the United States, in the chaotic and dynamic world that is likely to emerge from the present war, will be prepared to continue indefinitely to protect Canada without demanding a measure of active cooperation in return. It is a reasonable assumption that the United States will expect, and if necessary demand, Canadian assistance in the defence of this continent and this Hemisphere. Concrete steps such as the construction of the Alaskan Highway, the defensive development of the Pacific Coast and the Maritime Provinces, the co-ordination of Canadian and United States war material ... these are lines along which Washington is likely to require Canadian cooperation. If the United States is forced to defend the Americas against encroachments from across either Ocean, Canada will be expected to participate; thus the negotiation of a specific offensive-defensive alliance is likely to become inevitable.[17]

Indeed it would, and when Roosevelt telephoned Mackenzie King and invited him to Ogdensburg, New York in mid-August, King was only too pleased to go. The result of this meeting was the Ogdensburg Agreement, a simple statement that announced the creation of a Permanent Joint Board of Defence charged with beginning "immediate studies relating to sea, land and air problems . . . It will consider in the broad sense the defence of the north half of the Western Hemisphere."[18]

The Agreement was a logical extension of Roosevelt's pledge of 1938. What was striking about it, however, was that the Board was declared to be permanent. Seen in retrospect, the Agreement marked the shift from Canada as a British dominion to Canada as an American protectorate. Some people realized this at the time,[19] but in the general relief that Canada's safety was assured in the face of Axis power only the very foolish felt obliged to say so in public.[20] There was one very important, very cool response from abroad, however. Churchill wired King that

> I am deeply interested in the arrangements you are making for Canada and America's mutual defence. Here again there may be two opinions on some of the points mentioned. Supposing Mr. Hitler cannot invade us and his Air Force begins to blench under the strain, all these transactions will be judged in a mood different to that prevailing while the issue still hangs in the balance.[21]

Churchill's pique at Canada's scurrying to protect itself was understandable. But the British Prime Minister was wrong to assume that Canadian public opinion would permit the defences of Canada to be stripped so that aid could be sent to England without some guarantee of Canada's security. No Canadian government, charged above all with the defence of Canada, could have acted otherwise. The Ogdensburg Agreement, in addition, tied the United States closer to the belligerents, a positive gain for the Allied cause. In the long-run, however, Churchill was prophetic.

The post-Ogdensburg linkages between the two North American states developed apace. The PJBD began its meetings almost immediately and soon the Board was drafting plans and making recommendations to the two governments.[22] One of its suggestions, apparently advanced by the Canadian secretary to the PJBD, was that a Joint Committee should be appointed to report on the possibilities of increased economic coordination between Canada and the United States. This idea was extensively discussed within the Canadian government and with some Washington officials, including Berle, and it formed the subject of a formal Canadian note to the United States, delivered on March 17, 1941. "It is the belief of the Canadian Government," the aide-memoire stated, "that the promotion of economy and efficiency during the present period of crisis, the solution of the problems which will be posed during the period of transition from war to peace, and adequate and effective provision for the continuing requirements of hemisphere defence, all demand that early and detailed study be given to this question." The upshot was the establishment of the Joint Economic Committee in June, 1941. Its task was to study and report on the "possibilities of 1) effecting a more economic, more efficient and more coordinated utilization of the combined resources of the two countries in the production of defence requirements . . . and 2) reducing the probable post-war economic dislocations consequent upon the changes which the economy in each country is presently undergoing."[23] The Committee, like the Hyde Park agreement, was a Canadian initiative toward closer integration of the North American economy.

The Canadian aim in these critical months of 1940 and 1941 had been to bind the Dominion to the United States. In part this was a plain and simple desire for the protection that could be afforded by the American government. Part, too, was a clear desire to involve the United States more closely with a belligerent, to tie America and the Commonwealth closer together. To help Canada was to help Britain, and this was certainly the case with the Hyde Park Declaration, which ensured that Canada would not fall victim to an exchange shortage that could interrupt the flow of supplies to England.

In strictly Canadian terms, however, there were both assets and liabilities on the new balance sheet. The gains were in terms of security and the jobs, economic stability, and access to vital components that the new relationship with the United States brought. There was also a new influence in Washington. But Canada was also being linked inextricably into an American-dominated nexus, and its production and resources were increasingly coming to be thought of as joint assets. *The Canadian Forum* noted in June, 1941 that the Americans "are more and more tending to look upon the military and economic integration which is taking place between Canada and the United States as the starting-point. . . . They are hinting more and more openly that Canadian-American plans, military and economic, are not merely for the duration of the war."[25]

Even as the *Forum* wrote, however, the shift in American planning was in process. Talks with the British military had begun early in 1941, and joint planning was already far advanced. From the point of view of the War and Navy Departments in Washington it was much easier to negotiate with Britain alone rather than individually with Britain and her passel of Dominions. As a result when the Canadians tried in mid-1941 to secure U.S. permission to establish a military mission in Washington they were rebuffed. Repeated efforts were dealt with in a similar way, and it was not until July, 1942, that a full-fledged Canadian Joint Staff was created in Washington.[26] The hemispheric vision was gone after a year's existence. In its place was a global dream. Pearl Harbor forcibly fixed the new vision firmly in place.

For Canada the results would be pronounced. From being a vital link in the defence of the hemisphere in 1940-41, Canada had become a mere appendage of limited importance. The Canadian government had made agreements of far-reaching importance based on the continuance of an American hemispheric scheme, and now that scheme was dead. Roosevelt and King would still meet and talk in a friendly way, but no longer would the President feel obliged to deliver messages to London through the medium of Mackenzie King. He and Churchill met for the first time in August, 1941 off Newfoundland, a meeting at which the Canadian Prime Minister was prominent only by his absence. The realities had intervened.

The new Canadian position vis-à-vis the United States greatly concerned the Department of External Affairs, and Norman Robertson, the Under Secretary, prepared a long memorandum on the subject for the Prime Minister a few weeks after Pearl Harbour. Canadians, Robertson wrote, "have tended to take it for granted" that the United States "will always regard Canadian interests as a close second to their own and appreciably ahead of those of any third country." Now this was no longer so.

It is probably an inevitable consequence of the increasing involvement of the United States in the war and of its acceptance of leadership of the democratic cause that the President should tend more and more to deal directly with the Great Powers and find less time to spend on the specifically

Canadian aspects of American international relations. Canada naturally loomed much larger in the American scheme of things when the President and both political parties in the United States were thinking primarily in terms of continental and hemispheric defence. Now that the world war is joined on both oceans, the United States is, not unnaturally, inclined to take Canadian concurrence and support entirely for granted.

The result was a shift in the tenor of Canadian-American relations, a shift that Robertson believed to be "rather abrupt and not too tactfully handled." Part of the problem was caused by the scattering of responsibility for foreign affairs among a plethora of new agencies and offices in Washington and partly by the growing pressure there for a unification of Allied representation in the United States. Canadian matters were no longer always checked with the Department of State, as they had been before the war; and indeed the Department was rapidly declining in influence with the President at this time. Of course, contact between opposite members in various agencies in Ottawa and Washington was close and a useful aid to a speedy resolution of technical problems. But, Robertson argued, this gain was "offset by the loss ... of the preferred position Canada had gradually consolidated through long years of close and friendly collaboration with the President and the Department of State."

Equally important was the shift in the American perception of power. Before the war, Robertson claimed, the U.S. believed it could save the world by "its example, by minding its own business, pursuing a fair and friendly policy toward its neighbours ...." This era was now over and "we can see the United States turning everywhere to more direct and forceful methods of exerting its influence." This had been shown, for example, in the way the Americans had taken over the negotiations with Vichy France and in the way they had monopolized dealings with Japan before Pearl Harbor. The effect of this "new appreciation of the enormous strategic importance and strength of the United States" was a "new sense of . . . 'manifest destiny' and a corresponding disposition to take decisions and accept responsibilities. This change of attitude is very encouraging from the standpoint of the world in general but," Robertson warned, "it does imply quite an important modification of the special relationship in which Canada has hitherto stood with regard to the United States."

There were a host of examples that showed that the special relationship was gone. Robertson cited the "gradual assumption by the United States of hegemony in Newfoundland" as one and the negotiation of the Atlantic Charter by Roosevelt and Churchill alone as another. Equally important in his view was Canada's omission from the Anglo-American discussions of post-war commercial relationships then in progress although "the field of these negotiations is one in which, up until this year, Canada has taken a much greater initiative than any other part of the British Commonwealth."

Robertson was probably painting an idealized picture of the pre-1941 period, but that there was a shift in Canadian-American relations was clear. What was to be done? Probably the most able civil servant of his gene- ration, Robertson could only suggest that Canada upgrade its Legation in Washington to embassy status and appoint as ambassador an individual who would also sit in the Cabinet War Committee in Ottawa.[27] The first part of this recommendation was to be carried out in 1943 without noticeable effect. Quite likely nothing that Canada could have done would have achieved much. The United States was now well and truly launched on a search for world power as pronounced as the reluctance to accept binding commitments had been during the interwar years.

Curiously, just at the time that some Canadians were

beginning to worry about their declining relationship with Washington, the British were beginning to think that Canada's links with the United States were too close, that Ogdensburg and Hyde Park marked the seduction of Canada out of the empire and into the arms of America. Malcolm MacDonald, the British High Commissioner in Ottawa who was very close to Mackenzie King, noted that "There may be some danger that Mr. Mackenzie King will be inclined to associate Canada too closely as a North American country with the United States as distinct from the United Kingdom." King's friendship with the President worried MacDonald, but the High Commissioner concluded that King's loyalty to the Commonwealth was "paramount in his mind as it is in the minds of his fellow countrymen."[28] Other British ministers were by no means as certain. "Bobbetty" Cranborne, the Secretary of State for Dominion Affairs, worried often about Canada's too-close relationship with the United States, and in a 1942 minute to a file he observed that "I do not like feeling that [Canada's] closest contacts are with Washington in matters of national defence."[29]

What of Mackenzie King? His career has been based in part on his desire to create closer ties with the United States and to cut away the bonds that entangled Canada in the affairs of empire.[30] But as MacDonald properly assessed him, he was a sentimental imperialist, a devotee of the British connection, and an almost fawning courtier before British royalty. To King, however, Roosevelt was almost a monarch, and the correspondence from Prime Minister to President was sometimes almost embarrassing in its devotion. After a visit to Washington in May, 1942, for example, King wrote that "I could not, if I would begin to tell you how much I enjoyed its every hour and, particularly, the intimate personal talks with yourself."[31]

This kind of hyperbole aside, King was very capable of

assessing Canada's American problem realistically. He liked Roosevelt and admired him deeply,[32] and he knew that he could win important concessions for his country simply because his access to the President allowed Canada often to bypass the bureaucracy. In 1940, for example, he noted that "there is real purpose behind my seeing the President ... I can do more in one week spent to that end than might be accomplished in months by remaining at Ottawa."[33] Still, Roosevelt was not the United States. The Alaska Highway, begun in 1942, was one issue that impressed upon King the need to protect Canada's sovereignty against the Americans. The road, he told Malcolm MacDonald in March, 1942 "was less intended for protection against the Japanese than as one of the fingers of the hand which America is placing more or less over the whole of the Western hemisphere."[34] He told the same thing to another visitor: "it was not without some concern that ... I viewed the Alaska Highway and some other things growing out of the war, ... [and it] was clear to my mind that America has had as her policy, a western hemisphere control which would mean hemispheric immunity ... from future wars but increasing political control by U.S."[35] In Cabinet, King "held strongly to the view with one or two others that we ought to get the Americans out of the further development there [Norman Wells, N.W.T.], and keep complete control in our hands."[36] Again and again, King told his callers the same thing. With some it was what they wanted to hear, to be sure. He told the anglophilic Vincent Massey that "Canadians were looked upon by Americans as a lot of Eskimos,"[37] for example, but the refrain is so consistent that King certainly believed what he said.[38] Whether he did enough to counter American penetration is another question entirely.

King was not alone in feeling uneasy about American

policy, as a whole series of assessments penned in the Department of External Affairs in 1943 and 1944 make clear. H. L. Keenleyside, for example, had detected a coordinated American effort to obtain post-war advantages in Canada as a result of United States wartime expenditures in the Northwest. The American people, he argued, "have begun to think in terms of postwar advantage . . . a popular feeling in the United States that the Administration will be failing in its duty if it does not provide now for the acquisition of post-war profit from wartime expenditure in foreign countries."[39] Lester Pearson, the second-ranking officer in Washington, was similarly worried, and he regretted "that we should be so often forced into a position where we have to complain to the State Department about slights or injuries or omissions." There was another danger, Pearson added. "On instructions from Ottawa, we take a firm stand in Washington in opposition to certain United States demands. But as soon as pressure is exerted by the U.S. Government either here or in Ottawa, we give in . . . This kind of diplomacy, the strong glove over the velvet hand, has nothing to commend it."[40] The same kind of feeling was expressed by Escott Reid, a young and able nationalist who before the war had been one of the leading neutralists in Canada. Reid had served in Washington early in the war and now he was back in Ottawa. Some Canadians, he observed in a memo sent to Norman Robertson, were expressing the fear that Canada was becoming an adjunct of the United States "without the formalities of annexation" simply because the Americans were becoming more insistent about demanding and getting their own way. To many Americans, their participation in the war "is a favour which the United States is conferring on humanity and which carries with it the right to run things their own way." This was particularly true of recent dealings with Canada, Reid said. Before the war, a patronizing "Good Neighbour" attitude had not been shown to Canada but now it was, and one reason for this change was just plain aggressiveness. One example Reid cited dealt with an argument over wheat sales. The American Embassy in Ottawa had told the Deputy Minister of Trade and Commerce "that if we did not sell the wheat at the low price demanded by the United States they would be forced to announce publicly that because of Canada's decision the United States would have to cut down on wheat shipments to the United Kingdom and the U.S.S.R." The message was clear: Canada would have to be prepared for "energetic, aggressive and at times inconsiderate policies on the part of the Administration in Washington and as close neighbours we may see more of this than most other people."[41]

All these fears notwithstanding, however, the realities of geographical propinquity, of economic dependence, and of the potential problems of continental defence gave Canada little room for manoeuvre. The Cabinet War Committee finally decided in July, 1945 to maintain defence ties with the United States into the post-war world. The ministers' deliberations for more than a year had centred around successive drafts of a paper on "Post War Defence Arrangements with the United States," the major thrust of which was that the United States "may be expected to take an active interest in Canadian defence preparations in the future." The reason was clear: "Canada lies astride the overland route between the United States and the USSR." Any deterioration in Soviet-American relations would be embarrassing to Canada, the paper said, but in the event of any such embarrassment it was clear that Canada stood with the United States. As the paper also noted, "This closer tie-up with the United States need not conflict with the Canadian tradition of basing military policy and training upon British practice. However," the drafters of the report said, surely realizing the import of their words, "if Canada and the United States are to be efficient in the defence of North America, common experience between the national forces will be desirable."[42]

The government's decision was made, and so evidently was that of the informed public. This became very clear in 1945 when the Canadian Institute of International Affairs, its membership comprising virtually the entire Canadian foreign policy community, met at Kingston on May 26-27, 1945. The Canadian desk officer at the State Department in Washington, J. Graham Parsons, attended and addressed the meeting. His remarks and the reaction they received were reported to London by a British observer:

> There was a high degree of acceptance of the proposition that Canada's future political alignment would be with the United States, and only secondarily with the British Commonwealth ... The view ... was tactfully encouraged by Mr. Parsons ... He said that Canada's views and wishes exerted an influence on the United States administration out of all proportion to Canadian power, and added that on commercial policy Canada already enjoyed a consideration accorded to Great Powers alone. The enormous gratification of the company at this remark could not be concealed, and it apparently occurred to no one that it might be a bit exaggerated and of questionable validity in relation to the future.
>
> Mr. Parsons went on to describe as a source of some embarrassment to the United States the elasticity of the present system under which Canada's interests are presented sometimes through Canadian diplomatic channels and sometimes through London ... He said that the effect was that the State Department did not always know where Canada stood on particular issues.[43]

The shift was almost complete. Most Canadians now recognized that they lived in a North American nation and, although it would take a decade to become completely apparent, the Commonwealth tie was now in decay.

Two Canadian officials who spent much of the war in Washington summed it all up in an academic article written in 1945 that described the kind of cooperation that had existed in Washington:

> There has been the open exchange of confidence between the Americans and Canadians, the warm welcome, the freedom from formality, the plain speaking, and the all-pervading friendship. Neither is it easy to enumerate the conditions which made the high degree of co-operation possible. Co-operation was, of course, a sensible course to follow. It stood on its own merits. However, commonsense is not always able to prevail over sovereignty, and self-interest, and special national interests. That the course was followed, or at least adopted so readily and successfully is due in part to the friendly disposition that existed, attributable no doubt to our common background of language and culture, and to the close trade and industrial relationship: in part it is due to the fact that our approach to problems is similar.[44]

Canadians and Americans were almost the same.

Over the course of the next few years, the pressing demands of international politics would force Canadians and Americans still closer together. Canadian policy-makers generally wanted this and pressed for it, seeing certain advantages for Canada in it. Their caution remained, however, and eventually they would begin to seek with increasing desperation for new makeweights to the United States. The United Nations, the North Atlantic Treaty Organization, even finally the Commonwealth — all would be tried and found wanting. The links that had been forged during the war were too strong. Those were "the ties that bind."

CHAPTER SIX

CORPORAL PEARSON, GENERAL ACHESON AND THE COLD WAR[1]

The Second World War marked a watershed in foreign policy in both Canada and the United States. Before the war, both countries had been reluctant to participate in the diplomatic struggles in Europe, both feeling that once burned was more than enough. Both nations, of course, pursued trade with vigour, and on certain occasions and in certain circumstances both had entered into lengthy discussions with foreign powers. But it is fair to say that the mid-western distrust for the outside world was a common characteristic of the two nations.

The war altered everything. The United States was thrust on to the stage as the superpower with global responsibilities and problems, with a huge budget for arms and for aid, and with rapidly expanding interests. The shock of war to Canada was no less pronounced in proportion, and the cautious budgeting of the 1930s disappeared in a surge of confidence in Canadian arms, productive power and diplomacy. Both countries came out of the war untouched, strong, and increasingly convinced of mission. Formation of the United Nations, the Truman Doctrine, the creation of NATO, the Korean War — those were milestones on the road to a new era in international relations and in Canadian-American relations, too. As it reshaped the world, so this early postwar period altered the contours of bilateral relations on the North American Continent.

And no two men better capture the spirit of these years for their generation than Lester Pearson and Dean Acheson. Stout soldiers in the battle against Russian expansion and left-wing movements, they moulded North American public opinion on the great issues of the day. They were secular preachers in the postwar crusade against Communism, and although there were differences between them, as between any bishop and curate, there was no disagreement on the fundamentals of doctrine. In advancing and administering their policies, both were high-fliers within their governments; they were active, driving forces for forward action determined that .their countries seize every opportunity to assume the duties that power demanded.

In this endeavour, significantly, both received the support of their chiefs, Louis St. Laurent, first Secretary of State for External Affairs and then Prime Minister, and President Harry S Truman. Pearson and Acheson stood at the centre of political power within their governments, the closest of colleagues to the leader. The importance of this point can be underscored by supposing what the situation might have been had Franklin Roosevelt or Mackenzie King remained in authority and good health. Neither Acheson nor Pearson would have received the same free hand and both countries' foreign policy, in all likelihood, would have been more cautious.

Curiously, both Acheson and Pearson had roots in the other's country. Acheson's parents had met and married in Toronto, where his mother came from the established and wealthy Gooderham family. His father had attended the University of Toronto, served in the Queen's Own Rifles in

Thomas White (left), with Robert Borden and Sir Wilfrid Laurier, probably just before the outbreak of war.

The Imperial War Conference, May 1, 1917. Front row, left to right: Arthur Henderson, Viscount Milner, Lord Curzon, Andrew Bonar Law, David Lloyd George, Sir Robert Borden, W.F. Massey (P.M., New Zealand), Jan Christian Smuts.

The Signing of the first U.S. cheque to Great Britain, April 26, 1917. Left to right: Lord Cunliffe, Governor of the Bank of England; Sir Cecil Spring-Rice, British Ambassador to the U.S.; W.G. McAdoo; Sir Hardman Lever; Sir Richard Crawford; Oscar T. Crosby, Assistant Secretary of the U.S. Treasury.

Woodrow Wilson and his war administrators. Left to right, front: Benedict Crowell, Assistant Secretary of War; W.G. McAdoo, Secretary of the Treasury; Wilson; Josephus Daniels, Secretary of the Navy; Bernard Baruch, Chairman of the War Industries Board; standing: Herbert Hoover, Food Administrator; Edward N. Hurley, Chairman of the Shipping Board; Vance McCormick, Chairman of the War Trade Board; Harry A. Garfield, Fuel Administrator.

The King government's Cabinet War Committee, 1942. left to right, front: C.G. Power, T.A. Crerar, Mackenzie King, J.L. Ralston, J.L. Ilsley; standing: A.L. Macdonald, J.E. Michaud, C.D. Howe, L.S. St. Laurent.

HMCS Niagara, the former USS Thatcher, just a few days after transfer from the U.S. Navy. She was one of the fifty destroyers turned over in exchange for U.S. use of British bases, marking one of the early U.S. steps to belligerent status.

C.D. Howe, in 1943.

Women producing parts for Bren guns in an Ontario factory.

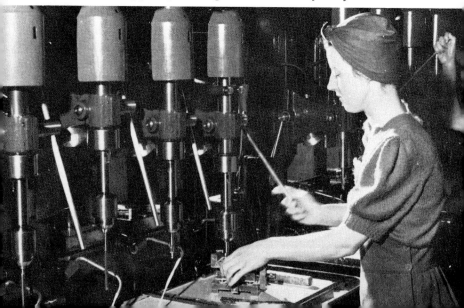

Quebec Conference, 1943. Anthony Eden, King, Roosevelt, Princess Alice, Cadogan, Bracken, Churchill.

B-24 Liberators on the assembly line of the Willow Run plant, Michigan.

U.S. Secretary of the Treasury Henry Morgenthau at Allied Headquarters in England, 1944.

St. Laurent with Vincent Massey in Ottawa, 1951.

U.S.A.

Pearson with Acheson and Eden.

Pearson, Eisenhower, U.N. Secretary-General Trygve Lie, and John Foster Dulles.

HOW TO KEEP HEALTHY

A 1949 (February) Ca-nadian Forum view Canada's entrance in NATO.

the North West Campaign of 1885, and become an Anglican clergyman. In 1892, just after his marriage, he accepted a post in Middletown, Connecticut, where Dean Acheson was born the following year. In his youth, Acheson frequently came to Toronto for visits with his mother's family, and even in Connecticut there were ritual ceremonies to mark the Queen's birthday, ceremonies in which the Union Jack would be raised and toasts offered. And his rites of passage to manhood were undergone in the bush of Northern Ontario where he worked for a summer on the construction of the Grank Trunk Pacific railway.[2]

Like Acheson, Pearson was a son of the manse. His family's roots were also in Toronto, and Pearson's preacher father held charges throughout Southern Ontario. "The first sixteen years of my life were spent in the Edwardian end of the Victorian era," Pearson recalled. "It was a time when we felt that God was in his heaven and all was well with our world. For a young Canadian that world was a very small part of a province, of a dominion, in an empire on which the sun was said never to set. And then in August, 1914 the armies moved, and it all ended."[3] Still in his teens, Pearson soon enlisted and served in Salonika and Britain. His military career was honourable though unglorious, but he at least had survived where so many of his contemporaries did not. After the war, through family connections, he took a menial job with Armour, the giant meatpackers in Chicago, an experience that persuaded him that his metier lay elsewhere. After Oxford and a stint of teaching history at the University of Toronto, he entered the Department of External Affairs at the end of the 1920s. For the next decade, he was a learner of the craft of diplomacy, progressing steadily upward through the ranks of the tiny department, making friends here, learning how to deal politely with the difficult there. Canadian policy was narrow, but there was some scope for a man of talent.[4]

Acheson's route to diplomacy was different. After Groton, Yale and Harvard Law, he moved almost instantly into the higher circles by being named a law clerk to Mr. Justice Brandeis. It was the best of entrées, and shortly thereafter Acheson was arguing cases before the International Court at the Hague as a member of a great and powerful Washington law firm. It seemed only natural for him to be asked by President Roosevelt to join the New Deal in 1933 as Under Secretary of the Treasury, and although this first experience in administrative politics was interesting, it was also unenjoyable, and before his first year was up Acheson had resigned on a point of principle over monetary policy.[5] He would not return to the government until 1941, when he joined the Department of State as Assistant Secretary of State.

Both Acheson and Pearson were well into their forties by 1939, both fully formed. Clearly Acheson was the tougher, more brilliant mind, the man with the best of connections who had begun at the top and remained there. He was a man of principle, an aristocrat by temperament and appearance. The contrast with Pearson was marked. The Canadian was able, no doubt about that, but he was a bureaucrat who had to sway with the winds. He could not afford to resign on a point of principle during the depression, and it is unlikely that such an idea would ever have occurred to him. His attitudes to policy questions were not very different from those that prevailed at Ottawa, and his letters and despatches home were carefully cut to fit his readers' preconceptions.[6] His greatest asset was his charm, a self-deprecating wit, and a neat turn of phrase, a sharp contrast to Acheson's excoriating, destructive sarcasm and polished, biting prose.

The careers of both were marked by professionalism. Pearson embodied the short-lived but already strong civil service tradition in Canada that had seen some of the ablest men of his generation leave the universities to join External Affairs or the Department of Finance. In the United States, top government posts were traditionally filled by men drawn from the upper reaches of corporation law, business and finance, a milieu into which Acheson fitted perfectly. This group of professionals in both countries, conceiving themselves to be part of an international governing class, shared the underlying confidence of a generation that had brought their countries through the Second World War, a confidence that they would lead the postwar world. Of course, Canadians shared this vision in a minor key. A colony a few years before, Canada did not possess the extraordinary global reach of American economic or military power, and the Canadian economy was increasingly dependent on regular and massive infusions of American capital. But this weakness was only relative, and in a world enfeebled by war, the Canadian high-fliers were determined to encourage Americans in their responsibility for world power as well as to participate themselves in the creation of the *Pax Americana*.

No less than the Truman administration, the Canadian leadership felt committed to the extension of American power in the fight against Communism. This was a fundamental premise for both Pearson and Acheson despite differences in detail and tactics. The roots of their attitude, of course, lay partly in the prewar years. "The generation which came to positions of leadership during the war," writes Gaddis Smith, "could never forget the behaviour of Hitler. . . . The image . . . seared itself on the eyes of all who fought him. When Hitler was gone, the image lingered."[7] Hitler and the Nazis were easily replaced in this image by Stalin and the Communists.

But if military power and collective security were required to avoid the mistakes of the past, the subversive ideology of Communism gave greater urgency still. Perhaps even more than Acheson, Pearson seemed to believe in a monolithic Communist conspiracy bent on revolutionary expansionism. In 1948, Pearson had argued that

> The chief menace now is subversive aggressive Communism, the servant of power politics. . . . [There are] no fire-proof houses in the atomic age, or little countries far away, like Czechoslovakia in 1938, whose fate means nothing to us. Our frontier now is not even on the Rhine or rivers further east. It is wherever free men are struggling against totalitarian tyranny, of right or left. It may run through the middle of our own cities, or it may be on the crest of the remotest mountain.[8]

For Pearson the central point was the "struggle of free, expanding progressive democracy against tyrannical and reactionary communism. . . ."[9] That did not sound too different from Acheson who said in 1950 that there could be "no moral compromise" with international Communism for "subversion, threats, and even military force" were integral to it.[10]

In this struggle, Pearson never questioned the moral basis of American leadership. Nor did he ever doubt that the Soviet Union bore sole responsibility for the Cold War, a view that he could put forcefully — and with an almost incredible naivete — as late as 1958:

> Western democratic governments have no aggressive or imperialistic designs. This is as true of the most powerful, the United States of America, as it is of, say Uruguay or Iceland. Indeed, Americans, though no Russian may ever believe it, are perhaps the least imperialistically minded people that ever achieved great power in the world. . . . Americans are not by nature or desire wandering empire builders. The "white man's burden" has little appeal for them, and the call of far places can be satisfied on their own continent. They are home-bodies, and their "westerns" give them an adequate if vicarious sense of adventure.[11]

But if Pearson greeted the overall thrust of American postwar policy with relief and enthusiasm, there were differences nonetheless. Pearson was much less nationalistic than Acheson and consequently much more interested in supranational institutions. In short, the Canadian was idealistic compared to Acheson who, accused of many things in his career, was never charged with a surfeit of idealism. Pearson had come to his beliefs early, and they were yet another product of the Hitlerian years. Sovereignty was an anachronism, he believed, and Canada had to be committed to internationalism. As early as 1941 he had said that "we may find it desirable to make adjustments in respect of some aspects of legal sovereignty in return for larger advantages. Such concessions do not, however, worry me. If we are to remove the recurring anarchy of war, *all* states will have to abandon some of the attributes of sovereignty in the interest of larger associations of nations."[12] The next year he intoned that "those political concepts 'self-determination' and 'sovereign rights', which were the guiding principles of the last peace, must be modified at the next peace conference in the light of . . . interdependence." Moreover, he urged, "Recognition of this interdependence may well, in turn, result in the grouping of small nations — of their own free will — around larger nations."[13] Indeed, according to Pearson, the small nations had a special obligation, for their fate during the 1930s had shown the hopelessness of neutrality and isolated independence. The cases of Belgium and Holland had proved to Pearson that "small states cannot rely on their own efforts for protection." They, Canada presumably included, "will have to subordinate their policies and their military plans to those of the larger powers."[14] Pearson's mind, therefore, influenced by conclusions drawn from the prewar years, was ready to accept the kind of aggressive leadership that Truman and Acheson offered in the Cold War years.

Logically enough, then, Pearson was thoroughly committed to the United Nations and to the founding of international political structures. He went to the San Francisco conference in 1945 filled with idealism about the future and determined that "San Francisco was to be no second Versailles" with harsh terms for the defeated. "For a few weeks," he recalled, "we thought we had scaled the heights and could see the promised land."[15] Later he recognized that "we expected much — too much — at San Francisco"[16] but it had all seemed possible then.

The Canadians were among the founding fathers of the United Nations, and clearly there was immense pride in Canada's contribution. For this reason, perhaps, the East Block under Pearson's direction became the UN's foremost supporter in the ensuing years. Certainly Pearson was a chief advocate of the international body, and the UN, as he reiterated often, was one of the cornerstones of Canada's foreign policy. Internationalism was in Pearson's hands the ideology of a pioneer in world political organization. It was an ideology which encouraged commitment to an administrative creation with which he strongly and persistently identified. It was more than official duty that motivated Pearson and his officers. "This work of organizing and strengthing the peace was more than an official concern of mine," Pearson said. "I was deeply involved personally."[17] It was heady stuff for a small town Ontario boy, the glitter of New York, a chance for the world stage. Who could fail to be tempted? And when policy, idealism and personal ambition coincided the temptations must have been very great indeed. For Pearson, and for other Canadians, the UN offered a double career. Success was possible not only in Ottawa but on the world stage as well. Dana Wilgress, another member of the Canadian delegation at San Francisco, recalled that "I had become so embroiled in the affairs of the United Nations that I began to consider it the best setting for my future work."[18]

How different from Dean Acheson. Once his youthful flirtation with the League of Nations had ended, Acheson never looked back to international political organizations as a desirable end. They could not be the centre piece of world peace or of American policy to him. Internationalism, if it was a viable concept at all, had to be concerned with economic and military matters. Acheson, moreover, was never as willing as Pearson to denounce national sovereignty, even in flights of rhetoric. American power, in his view, was what would bring peace, not the UN. The lesson to be learned from the 1930s was that a strong American economic and military machine was essential. "The Second World War," Acheson's recent biographer writes, "represented a second chance for the United States to exercise military power, not to achieve utopia through collective security."[19]

Acheson became more outspokenly critical of the United Nations in his later years, particularly after the fiasco at Suez in 1956,[20] but his views were evident early on. "I am often told that the way to solve this or that problem," he explained in 1946,

> is to leave it to the United Nations. But it seems to me inescapable that if they are, or we hope will be, united, they are still nations and no more can be expected of this forum for political ajdustment than the sum total of the contributions. If these are wise and steadfast and supported by strength determined to organize peace, the results will be good. But, in the Arab proverb, the ass that went to Mecca remained an ass, and a policy has little added to it by its place of utterance."[21]

Far more germane for Acheson were matters of international economic and monetary policy. International adjustments were important, of course, but "These tasks are more deeply affected by how we and others master the intricacies of the production and movement of food and other goods, with how successfully we deal with labor problems and inflation, with credits, with the wise use of natural resources. They may even involve the most national of all problems — the efficiency of the administrative and legislative processes." He understood the Pearsonian argument about the dangers of nationalism, but Acheson's response was characteristic: "It may be so, but to a sinking heart there comes the admonition of Old Hickory at the battle of New Orleans ... 'Boys, elevate them guns a little lower.' It may be that the way to solve a difficult problem is to transfer one's own attention to an insoluble one. But I doubt it."[22]

Even NATO was no different. "There is no substitute for strength at the center," Acheson said. "Alliances are important ... But it is equally important, if not more important, that there be strength at the center of these groups — the strength of the United States, its economic strength, its military strength, which will, in itself, breed strength at the periphery of our associations."[23]

Given Acheson's attitudes, it is completely understandable than Mike Pearson should have achieved a *persona* as a man of peace of a kind that Acheson could not — and would not have wanted. Pearson did this without sacrificing his national identity for he managed to reconcile to himself the ambiguities of nationalism and internationalism. "To me," Pearson said, probably expressing the view of a whole generation of Canadians, "nationalism and internationalism were two sides of the same coin. International co-operation for peace is the most important aspect of national policy."[24] More, internationalism would serve peculiarly Canadian national needs as well. "It helped us to escape the dangers of a too exclusively continental relationship with our neighbour without forfeiting the political and economic advantages of that inevitable and vitally important association." In addition, Pearson argued, "the broad and active internationalism" of those days "strengthened internal unity."[25]

Ambiguities and practical problems disappeared in the flow of rhetoric. External activity strengthened internal unity; internationalism supported nationalism; interdependence maintained independence; continental arrangements strengthened regional alliances; the drive for Canadian status and power contributed to world peace. As Pearson wrote in his characteristic way,

> Canada's true national interests were in no way sacrificed to, or prejudiced by, our international activities. On the contrary, these interests were strengthened. Indeed, in few countries is there less likely to be a conflict between national interests and international policy, since in few are the requirements of interdependence so closely related to the maintenance of independence. I believe that this role, played not to spread ourselves or to gain prestige, but to discharge our proper international responsibilities, strengthened our feeling of national pride. This, in turn, contributed to national unity and to a deeper sense of national identity. We had come of age. The voice of Canada was now being heard.[26]

To Dean Acheson, this would have been typical Canadian woolly moralizing. Nationalists today would bitterly argue that Pearson traipsed around the world while the Americans bought up Canada. And even Pearson himself finally recognized that his concerns in the years after 1945 did not include American investment and cultural penetration as they might have. He later noted this subject's omission from Louis St. Laurent's Gray Lecture which, in 1947, had laid down the fundamentals of postwar Canadian foreign policy. And he commented that "This omission, no doubt, was occasioned by the fact that we were not as conscious of any threat from these pressures in 1947 as we became later. We had, I think, more pride in our country and a greater faith in its future. We were more self-confident, less fretful."[27] The explanation is interesting in itself and curious, but the belief, it seems clear, was sincerely held.

And it was predominant in Parliament, too, where there

was a fairly clear consensus on the need to beat back Communism. This was the "golden" age of Canadian foreign policy[28] and Pearson, like his counterpart in the United States, could preach the idea of bipartisan foreign policy. It was, after all, consistent with his idea that activism abroad would bring unity at home. And in his first public address as a politician in 1948, he said that "we are all Canadians, or should be, before we are Liberals, Conservatives, or CCFers, and before we are Quebeckers or Manitobans. So we should face the outside world with a united front. Politics, it has been said by an American leader, should end at the water's edge."[29]

Acheson must have envied Pearson the comparative political ease he had in shaping the foreign policy consensus. He had bitter political enemies among conservative Republicans and the separation of powers in the American system greatly complicated his task. As Canadians so often observed, with no little air of superiority, a babel of raucous and contradictory voices frequently echoed from Washington, and Congress required as much watching as the White House in the policy-making process. Acheson's response in part was to resort to simplification and overdramatization of the Communist threat — manipulation and deception, some called it — and this, of course, only compounded his difficulties. In this divisive climate, Acheson could hardly become the popular and much-admired figure that Pearson was and has remained on the Canadian scene.

There were other factors, of course, Pearson, a product of the small-town Ontario of the early twentieth century, seemed a familiar figure, unpretentious, one of the boys. Not Acheson. Although born in a small town, he seemed too much the representative of an almost alien culture and tradition to mid-western America. The Groton-Yale-Harvard corporation lawyer image didn't wash in

Ohio and Nebraska. The policies Acheson represented also seemed to be going too far too fast.

The key element in the tough line with Russia was the North Atlantic Treaty, and there could be no better example of the divergence of thought and technique between Acheson and Pearson than in their differing interpretations of what NATO was and was meant to be. The sticking point was Article 2, a seemingly harmless pledge that the signatories of the Treaty

> will contribute toward the further development of peaceful and friendly international relations by strengthening their free institutions, by bringing about a better understanding of the principles upon which these institutions are founded, and by promoting conditions of stability and well-being. They will seek to eliminate conflict in their international economic policies and will encourage economic collaboration between any or all of them.

Article 2 was a Canadian initiative, and consequently the struggle for it looms large in Pearson's memoirs while it scarcely figures in Acheson's except as an irritant that required minor adjustment. For Acheson, an annoyance; for Pearson an article of faith and the touchstone of postwar Canadian foreign policy.

From the start Pearson and his followers in the Department of External Affairs wanted NATO to be something more than just another military alliance, "purely negative in character." There had to be provision "for peacetime co-operation in economic, social and cultural fields." If it was to last, the alliance had to be built on more than "just military co-operation."[30] The goal, in fact, was for "a genuine Atlantic Community, organised on a supra-national basis."[31]

And yet, surprisingly, from the start Pearson's crusade for Article 2 was almost his alone. In the summer of 1947, Pearson approved speeches that ran ahead of government policy,[32] and with his Minister he tried to counter Mackenzie King's caution on this and all foreign policy matters. Furthermore, there were skeptical reactions to talk about economic and political integration in the Finance and Trade and Commerce Departments, and even from within External Affairs. Perhaps it was to avoid internal criticism that Pearson confined discussion about NATO to a tiny group within his Department.[33]

To Pearson, the threat from the Communists was not so much that of military aggression as of subversion. This was a threat to which Article 2 would speak directly. It would also serve the additional purpose of persuading those doubters among the Canadian population that NATO was not just about guns. It could help cement Canada's ties with France, something that might ease Quebec fears about military entanglements. Pearson admitted this quite frankly later:

> One reason for our stand on this was, admittedly, political. We did not think that the Canadian people, especially in Quebec, would whole-heartedly take on far-reaching external commitments if they were exclusively military in character; nor should they be asked to do so. These domestic considerations . . . were reinforced by our dediction . . . to the grand design of a developing Atlantic community.[34]

And Article 2, in Pearson's view, was an opportunity to achieve the longstanding Canadian goal of Atlantic reconciliation, to put a peculiarly Canadian stamp on the international process.

To Dean Acheson, out of public life between July, 1947 and January, 1949 all this was nonsense. On his return to office as Secretary of State, "He impatiently dismissed our concern with non-military cooperation," writes Pearson, " . . . as typical Canadian moralizing that meant 'next to nothing.'"[35] Worse, this Canadian do-goodism threatened more important objectives and needs. The Senate, Acheson wrote in *Present at the Creation*, was opposed to clauses in the Treaty "that posed serious constitutional complications in federal-state relationships." Even supporters in the Senate "saw it threatening our treaty ... for no important benefit. I agreed."[36] Pearson could appreciate this problem, too. "We were in the old familiar position of being at one end of a double negotiation between the State Department and the other countries on the one hand, and the US Senate Foreign Relations Committee on the other."[37]

But Canadian domestic needs had to be served, too, and Pearson got Prime Minister St. Laurent to appeal directly to Truman. This produces a more amenable attitude in the State Department and the result was a compromise redrafting of Article 2. Acheson was convinced that it had been rendered harmless, but Pearson, ever the optimist, was certain it had been strengthened. But what is most striking in this episode is that Canada could get any such clause written into the Treaty at all. Hume Wrong, the Canadian negotiator, had even reported at one point that "We are now the only party to the negotiation that really favours the inclusion of anything in the Treaty about social and economic collaboration."[38] To succeed in the face of such opposition and apathy is a commentary on Pearson's influence at the time; to have persisted in the face of such disinterest is a demonstration both of his commitment to the idea and of his worries about Canadian public opinion.

In the final analysis, however, Acheson was right and Pearson was wrong. "The plain fact ... is that NATO is a military alliance," Acheson wrote later. "Its purpose was and is to deter and, if necessary, to meet the use of Russian military power or the fear of its use in Europe. ... Perhaps to avoid this stigma, Canadian draftsman had Article 2 inserted in the treaty. ... but despite studies by two groups . . . guided by Canadians, no promising areas were discovered."[39] That was cruel, perhaps, and it failed to take into account the obstacles that Acheson himself had put in the way of implementing Article 2. But it was true, and Pearson had to admit it: "Article 2 remained virtually a dead letter for substantive action on economic matters. . . . The reality is that the spirit to implement the economic aspects . . . was *never* there and that an economic basis for the realization of its larger political goal was never created. And, perhaps, it simply took me too long to realize this."[40]

What can one say about such a disarming admission of failure? A misguided effort out of excessive idealism? Perhaps so. But then idealism is an honourable failing; indeed, it is the only failing Pearson is willing to admit in a memoir marked by a genial rigidity. Failing from excessive idealism is almost a guarantee of a sentimental triumph, and while Acheson's reputation declines in the current "re-visioning" of the postwar years, the Pearson legacy remains in high esteem. "I remained on the side of the angels, however remote they were," wrote Pearson, a mischievous smile no doubt crossing his face.[41] Dean Acheson could not have said it better.

As Article 2 symbolized, Canadians wanted to achieve some separate identity in policy in the immediate postwar years, even while they championed the basic thrust of American initiative. They offered no fundamental alternatives to Truman administration policies. There was, it seems, no one in External Affairs to advocate spheres of influence or cautious policies toward Europe. The high-fliers had the stage almost to themselves, and though they hoped to find in the UN a kind of independent purchase in an increasingly bipolar world, they never emerged successfully from the American shadow.

The presentation of NATO's Article 2 and the UN to

the Canadian public was one of the outstanding selling jobs of the day. As a result, Canadians still feel themselves to be in company with Lester Pearson "on the side of the angels" in the origins of the Cold War. But the issues of the 1940s no longer seem to be as clear as they did then. Blacks and whites are fading into greys, and it is not too much now to say that the United States has to share responsibility for the tensions of those years. Canadian policy-makers were not remote from those issues; they eagerly joined the forces of "progressive democracy" and trumpeted the mission of North American liberalism. They never intended that it should be otherwise; Corporal Pearson willingly enlisted in the Acheson volunteers. It is difficult to believe that if External Affairs had taken over the State Department the results would have been much different.

CHAPTER SEVEN

LOOKING BACK AT THE COLD WAR

Contention over the present and future is always accompanied by contention over the past. Jousting partisans search for legitimacy and lineage, and Clio is called upon to justify both continuity and change. But even ransacking the past for rhetorical ammunition sometimes produces benefits. It sharpens awareness of the fact that we walk into the future backwards, and it heightens appreciation for the historical roots of current policies and institutions. Most important, such debates can lead in the end to a more objective and scholarly reconstruction of the past for its own sake. And out of such reconstruction and revision can come meaning and significance unknown to either historical actors in the past or to ideological partisans in the present.

If the historical reconstruction is still incomplete, the process of revision for American policy during and after the Second World War is in full swing. Historians have reflected the widespread disillusionment with American policy in the 1960s, and the vast upheaval in American society and culture has left its mark on their writings. But the critical questioning had been underway well before Viet Nam; William Appleman Williams and C. Wright Mills attacked the prevailing orthodoxies in the 1950s.[1] In addition, many of the questions spring from the writings of contemporary Cold War critics themselves. The views of dissenters like Robert Taft, I. F. Stone and James P. Warburg are being rediscovered and re-assessed, and their stock is climbing as the moral legitimacy of the Truman-Acheson policy comes under academic attack.[2] But whatever its origins, the revisionist critique has opened Pandora's box and questions that once seemed settled are alive again. The postwar goals of American policy, the goals that once were almost self-evidently good and proper, now seem tarnished. Some complain as Robert Taft did in 1950 that "The line between imperialism and idealism becomes very confused in the minds of those who operate the system."[3]

The relationship between idealism and the calculation of economic self-interest in the American policy of those years is, of course, central to the debate. Canadians, long accustomed to a tradition of state support for business enterprise and exports, may be less shocked to discover connections between the rhetoric of humanitarian aid to postwar Europe and the needs of farmers and businessmen for export markets. But a generation of sensitive American college students have not been so hardened, and the discovery that business needs intertwined with the unselfishness of the Marshall Plan, for instance, has been shattering, even though Americans were told at the time that the Marshall Plan served American economic ends.

Equally difficult to believe for most Americans — and perhaps for most Canadians, too — is the thought that the extension of American power in the Cold War years was neither as innocent nor as accidental as once portrayed. Perhaps the kind of mentality so chillingly revealed in *The Pentagon Papers* had its roots in an earlier time. The cult of toughness, which reached a kind of apotheosis along the

New Frontier, was, after all, borne of the wartime
experience. Many Americans left their country in 1941
"when America was merely the world's hope" and came
home again in 1945 convinced that it was now "the
world's necessity."[4] Some liberals who had worried during
the war about a growing alliance between the military and
big business and the possibilities of a garrison state became
the ideologues of the anti-Communist crusade of the late
1940s. Nor was this trend confined only to the United
States. Canadian liberalism shared a somewhat similar fate,
and Frank Underhill, a democratic socialist in the 1930s
and 1940s, could by October, 1950 defend the United
States and its acts with a fervour that Dean Acheson might
have admired.[5] But if the original questioning was
submerged by the avalanche of support for the
Truman-Acheson policy, it has surfaced again in an
exploration of the roots of the "military-industrial
complex" and the role of business, military and
government groups in national decision-making.

Questions have also been raised about the nature of the
anti-Communist crusade. Some have suggested that the
Truman administration exaggerated fears of an expansive
Russia in order to weaken opposition to a forward foreign
policy. And did the United States do all it could to reach
agreement with the Soviet Union on the control of atomic
development? Or were offers made that the Russians could
only refuse? General McNaughton, Canada's representative
at the United Nations, for instance, apparently regarded
the final American nuclear control plan (the Baruch plan)
as "insincerity from beginning to end."[6]

And what of Russian policy in these postwar days?
Historians are now beginning to give credence to the idea
that the Soviet Union really was more interested in the
security of its borders than in revolutionary expansion.
One of the insuperable obstacles to settling this question,

of course, is the lack of Russian sources, yet in retrospect the Russians may have been more conservative than many policy-makers were willing to admit at the time. At the very least, one can argue that United States policy must share some responsibility for the mutual hostility. It is a point, less broadly based, but not unlike one made by a Canadian observer at the time:

> Russia and the Western democracies bear a common responsibility for the present crisis. Moscow's truculent diplomacy and isolation has done disservice to Russia's search for peace and security. It has been a block to world co-operation. The West has done much to increase Russia's sense of insecurity and has offered little assistance to Russia in its Reconstruction tasks.[7]

These complex and still relatively unexplored issues can scarcely be settled here. Nor is it possible to review the substantial differences of purpose, method and conceptualization among the contributors to revisionist literature. Our purpose instead is to reflect on the implications of revisionism for a reassessment of Canadian foreign policy from 1945 to 1952, and for this it is enough simply to illustrate the general nature of the revisionist thrust by a closer look at two of the best contributions to the field, impressive in range, scope and analytical power: Gabriel Kolko's *The Politics of War: The World and United States Foreign Policy 1943-1945*, New York, 1968, and Joyce and Gabriel Kolko, *The Limits of Power: The World and United States Foreign Policy, 1945-54*, New York, 1972.

One of the most prolific American historians of his generation, Kolko is no stranger to revisionism. His early works analyzed the American economic structure and the nature of the state in the Progressive era and radically attacked the textbook views. The origins and functions of the state in American society are indeed central to Kolko's work on both domestic and foreign policy and his theoretical position on this point is worth noting at the outset. Kolko argues in a variety of books and articles that the federal bureaucracy, including its military component, emerged in its modern form as essentially a dependent variable of the country's underlying economic structure. The relationship, however, was not that of the classic formulation of monopoly capitalism breeding a centralized state administration. On the contrary, Kolko argues, American federal agencies and departments grew in response to a capitalism unable to rationalize itself. Public bureaucratic power has historically been derived, not primary, power and thus the state has not been a neutral referee in the struggle for wealth and power. In both domestic and foreign policy, he says, it has registered the structural needs of a capitalist economy. American government is not simply under the control of private interests, though their influence is strongly represented through the members of banks, financial institutions and corporate law firms who join the government in top administrative posts. More fundamentally, Kolko suggests that certain policies are likely to be followed in keeping with the structural needs of the economy irrespective, say, of the government's recruitment policy. This thesis, substantially more complex than portrayed here, is open to a number of questions, not the least of which is its tendency to deny the state and its managers any real autonomy and to minimize the interest group conflicts among them. Nevertheless, it is a theory and philosophy of history that confronts the reader of the Kolko books, not simply historical narrative. And it is well to remember that argument on one level will not necessarily settle debate on the other.[8]

But what is Kolko telling us about American foreign policy during and after the Second World War? In these two books, the United States is no selfless white knight pouring out its treasure in Lend-Lease and the Marshall Plan for the general good. Nor is it a nation obsessed with fears of Communism and acting irrationally in the face of the bogeyman. Not at all. In Kolko's view, the United States is a nation like the others, interested above all in the advancement of its own interests. American policy-makers and American businessmen, convinced and certain of the correctness of their analysis, knew full well what they were doing as they tried to restructure the world so as to advance their country's economic interests. And they knew, too, that the fear of Communism was a useful tool that could be used abroad to secure concessions and at home to persuade a sometimes balky Congress to go along with their intentions. As Kolko argues,

> It was often politically convenient for America's leaders to fix the blame for capitalism's failures on the cautious men in the Kremlin. . . . If, in the end, all of Washington's postwar leaders superficially attribute to one cause — Russia — the justification for everything they wish to do, it is only because such a style of explanation becomes critical to the very conduct and future of an American foreign policy for which these men have yet to find domestic legitimation and enthusiasm.[9]

In this not untypical Kolko quotation, a series of contentious theses are advanced in a matter of fact way, including the idea that the Communists were cautious, that the United States used the Communist scare for its own purposes, and that the American public was less than enthusiastic at first about the direction its leaders were taking the country.

Kolko argues that the United States administration after 1945 created phoney war scares and on several occasions rejected out of hand peace overtures from the Soviet Union. He argues, too, that American military expenditures remained relatively low until after the beginning of the Korean War, and even industrialists who might have been expected to welcome large defence expenditures were unenthusiastic. The United States, Kolko maintains, "spent about what it could afford on the military establishment . . . and as much as it thought the real, as opposed to publicized, threat of Soviet power and policies warranted to maintain its decisive military supremacy."[10]

This assessment of Soviet weakness is basic to the argument. The Soviets were on the defensive, in Kolko's view, desperate to keep a buffer between Germany and Russia, desperate to keep the aggressive, capitalist West at bay. Virtually all Soviet actions in the immediate postwar period were of this character, Kolko argues, including the seizure of power in Czechoslovakia, an event that Kolko attributes more to the incompetent and inept manoeuvering of Czech conservative politicians than to a world-wide conspiracy of militant Communism. Even the Korean War appears in Kolko's work in a different light. Syngman Rhee is the villain of the piece, and if this now is almost conventional wisdom, few will fail to be surprised by Kolko's variations on the theme. The South Koreans fell back before inferior North Korean forces, Kolko argues in a particularly provocative section, in a deliberate attempt to commit deeply the Americans. Their goal, of course, was the eventual forcible unification of the peninsula under Southern control.

The overall argument in Kolko's foreign policy studies rests on economic foundations. Here the main enemy of the United States is London, and the major economic goal is the destruction of the sterling bloc and Commonwealth preferences. When Lend-Lease was offered during the war, for example, one of the conditions demanded by American negotiators was an end to empire trade preferences, and this theme persisted into the postwar period. When an American loan was finally offered to the desperate British in 1946, it was less than London had expected, the terms were substantially stiffer, and the intention was clearly to benefit the United States as much as it was to help the British: lend them money so they can buy our goods. The same story recurs when the Marshall Plan is discussed, although in 1948 the American goal was also to prop up Western Europe against the threat of Communism. Not against a Soviet invasion, however; rather, the threat as perceived in Washington was from internal subversion or, worse, a democratic Communist victory at the polls. The formation of NATO was similarly based, Kolko claims, and was not primarily directed at the Soviet Union. It was "much more the outcome of Europe's desire to prevent a resurgent Germany from yet again disturbing the peace, to which the United States added its desire to strengthen Western Europe's ability to cope with internal revolt as well as to sustain a psychological mood of anti-Soviet tension that the administration thought functional." The "real Communist danger in Western Europe was internal."[11]

The differences between the received version of postwar foreign policy and Kolko's interpretation of it are striking. The characters are the same and the main events remain. But everything else is altered and the world is stood on its ear.

One need not agree with all aspects of Kolko's brilliant argumentation to realize that any shift in interpretation of United States policies during the Cold War poses questions about the nature of postwar Canadian goals as well. Canadian and American leaders interacted on the major issues of their day, and if our perceptions of the behaviour of the major actor change, we must adopt a new angle from which to appraise the supporting players. If Canadian leaders are at one point to be congratulated for welcoming U.S. internationalism in the fight against Russia, what is to be said once the aims and methods of that struggle are brought into question? Of course, this works both ways. A reassessment of Canadian policy could raise questions about the current revisionist critique of American policy. If Canadian leaders acted on a roughly similar perception of Russian expansionism, and not one owed to manipulation from Washington, then perhaps the American leadership was not uniquely Machiavellian or obtuse. If Canadian leadership again displayed the same thrust for foreign markets, then perhaps the issue is less American policy than capitalism in general. The need clearly is for greater international perspective on the origins of the Cold War.

There have been Canadian critics of American policy, but in general their concerns have been less with the kind of issues raised here than with the more narrowly conceived issue of determining the influence of American pressure on Canadian policy and policy-makers.[12] This is important, but our intent is to pursue the angle of vision offered by revisionists like the Kolkos to explore the ways in which Canadian methods and goals can be reinterpreted.

But first, what is the traditional version of Canadian foreign policy during these years? It usually goes something like this: Despite the obstructions thrown up by the near senile Mackenzie King, Canadian policy-makers soon realized that the United Nations was not going to function as the collective security guarantor to world peace. The blame for the collapse of the hopes of the war years clearly rested on the Soviet Union, and as early as the summer of 1947 Canadian diplomats were calling for the formation of a western alliance. Planning was spurred by the rape of Czechoslovakia early in 1948, and in 1949 NATO was finally created, in large part a tribute to the skill of Canadian diplomacy. When war broke out in Korea in June, 1950 Canada participated loyally despite some misgivings over American tactics. In the new situation resulting from the Korean War and its revelations about the Soviet willingness to use force, the government despatched substantial numbers of troops to Europe. In addition to these military measures, Canada contributed heavily to the recovery of Western Europe with mutual aid and with loans at low interest. All in all, this almost-authorized version goes, Canadian policy is at one with virtue. The old isolationism was dead. The new era of involvement had begun.[13]

How much was this political involvement owed to economic need? Canadian trade before the war and during it had been very dependent on the British market. Agriculture, in particular, was kept afloat by British sales, and if this market were lost or if the British became so insolvent as to be unable to keep up their orders, Canada's only major market would be the United States, a disquieting prospect. "The only long-run solution compatible with our national independence," wrote Professor Maurice Lamontagne in a very persuasive argument in 1948, "consisted in extending adequate aid to our traditional European customers."[14]

Similar reasons had been used to justify the $1 billion "gift" to Britain in 1942 and the huge Mutual Aid appropriations of the subsequent war years. A loan of $1.25 billion followed in 1946, a staggering sum of money that was more than double the entire federal budget in 1939 and fully one-third of the amount loaned to Britain by the United States that year. In addition almost $500 million more was loaned by the Canadian government to other Western European trading partners.

The arguments advanced in 1946 for the British loan were explicitly those of self-interest, arguments that might astonish American revisionists by their unabashed frankness. The leaders of all the parties accepted this reasoning, including M. J. Coldwell of the CCF. John

Bracken, the Leader of the Opposition and Progressive Conservative party chief, said, for example, that the loan "was essential to the preservation of the Canadian economy as we see it to-day. Ours is an export economy; we are more than any other country dependent upon foreign nations for a market for our products."[15]

Canada then had — and recognized — an enormous stake in maintaining Europe as a free market for its goods. Trade with Eastern Europe was negligible but very extensive with the North Atlantic nations, and self-interest was clear. And if the Americans were prepared to negotiate toughly with their desperate friends, so, too, were we. In December, 1947, for example, the British tried to back out of some foodstuff contracts with Canada and were sharply rebuffed by Prime Minister King and his negotiators. There was no gratitude among nations, Mackenzie King harrumphed in his diary, and if the British went back on their contracts "we will have to cancel all and let our farmers and others sell wherever they wish, to whatever countries they wish."[16] But that was not really King's wish. At least two fears constrained him on this issue: a domestic political concern that the Opposition would accuse him of selling out the British to join the Americans, and an international concern that division between Canada and the United Kingdom would only play into the hands of Communist propagandists.[17] Bargaining, however, by no means disappeared from the ultimate adjustment process.

Despite King's caution about giving the Tory opposition an easy political issue, the government did have to work out a series of economic arrangements with Washington in the immediate postwar years. King baulked at the idea of free trade, but he did accept other arrangements that raised serious questions about the degree of economic independence that remained to the Dominion. At issue in 1947 was a serious dollar exchange crisis. The unexpectedly slow rate of British recovery had forced the United Kingdom to draw on the Canadian loan very quickly, and at the same time the high level of Canadian consumer spending produced an unprecedented flow of American imports into Canada with serious results on Canada's U.S. dollar reserves. From May, 1946 the Canadian holdings dropped from $6.17 billion to $700 million in April, 1947 and then to $480 million on 30 November, 1947.[18] The result was a series of measures to cut imports and to reduce tourist spending abroad in the hope that the drain could be checked. Ironically, on November 17, 1947, the same day that the restrictions were announced, Mackenzie King announced that Canada had signed the General Agreement on Trade and Tariffs. Among other things, GATT reduced tariffs on seventy percent of American imports and similarly lowered U.S. barriers to Canadian products. The net effect was to spur resource development in Canada and to weaken protection afforded to domestic manufacturers. The short term measures against imports were important, but they were far exceeded by the long term implications of the General Agreement on Trade and Tariffs.

In this state of affairs, the Americans could afford to be generous when Canadians tried to win some benefits under the Marshall Plan arrangements. It was not aid they were after, but the right to have Marshall Plan dollars spent by Europeans for Canadian goods. And, of course, any general European recovery would enhance Canadian trading prospects.[19] What this meant, put into cold political terms, was that Canadian leaders became firm advocates of American aid to Europe, and Canadian publicists became just as anxious as the Truman administration to have Congress go along with an aggressive and generous policy. Many of the Canadians were as interested as the American policy-makers in economic multilateralism and as distrustful of arguments for economic and political isolationism and cautious systems of trade by barter.[20] And one usually knowledgeable commentator even argued that Canadian measures of November, 1947 were premised on the assumption that Marshall Plan aid would come to Canada as soon as Congress put up the funds.[21] How long austerity lasted for Canada, in other words, was dependent on how much Marshall Plan aid flowed Canada's way.

Although Canadian exports to the United States increased in 1948 to help right the balance,[22] the Marshall Plan played a crucial role, as government officials willingly acknowledged.[23] By April, 1949 fully $706 million had been spent in Canada for the Europeans, and soon the barriers erected in November, 1947 were down, soon American capital was flowing north once more, soon the Korean War would spur the rearmament of the West and Canadian prosperity would return. All that must be said on the issue of European aid is that Canadian economic needs contributed substantially to a foreign policy that converged at very much the same point reached by Washington decision-makers. The situation north of the 49th parallel, however, did put Canada into a double dependency, and it also produced the peculiar argument that aid to Europe, whether from Canada or the United States, lessened Canadian dependency on American markets. American money, by this reasoning, could be used to purchase Canadian economic independence, a piece of syllogistic reasoning not without flaws.

But as one very perceptive Canadian analyst pointed out at the time, there is more to economics than just economics. "Even if the problem is primarily economic," Maurice Lamontagne said of Canada's international situation, "it is much wider in scope and it cannot be analysed exclusively in economic terms. Its political and even cultural aspects should not be neglected, because they may have an important bearing on its solution. The methods by which our nation will reach a more stable position," he said, "must be derived from economics, but they cannot be appraised on purely economic grounds without considering their political or social implications."[24]

Economics demanded cooperation with the United States and support for European recovery, but the convictions and aspirations of the Department of External Affairs would not have settled for less in any event. Here was a reinforcing element for an activist foreign policy. Involvement had a symbolic quality to it as an explicit rejection of past policies of delay and evasion, quasi-neutrality, and "Parliament will decide." To press vigorously for a policy, almost any policy, was a positive good simply because it was so different from what had prevailed a few years earlier. Mackenzie King was far more cautious than the men in External Affairs, and he clashed with them on a variety of issues in the immediate postwar years. He was as convinced as any of the Department's officers that the Russians were a threat, but he still hoped that the diplomats would rein in their world-wide aspirations. "Canada's role was not that of Sir Galahad to save the whole world," King complained in December, 1947, "unless we are in a position to do it."[25] Clearly Canada was not in such a position, and the Prime Minister "felt that a great mistake was being made by Canada being brought into situations in Asia and Europe of which she knew nothing whatever, of interfering with Great Powers without realizing the consequences."[26] This cautious realism about the limitations of Canadian power seems better founded in retrospect than it did to many at the time.

But King was old and terribly tired, worn down by the strain of the war, and dependent on his already chosen successor, Louis St. Laurent. And when the Quebec lawyer was made Secretary of State for External Affairs in 1946 the die was cast. Very often thereafter King's hesitations, his querulous questions about Lester Pearson's adventurist policies, his skepticism about the United Nations, and his deep-seated concern to protect Canadian autonomy could be overridden. Unlike the men around him, King realized that withdrawal could sometimes be more liberating than commitment and participation. And he was afraid of American power. For a man who all his life had been accused by his political opponents of continentalist predilections, King was surprisingly vehement in his feelings. It was not that he was anti-American. Some of his best friends, after all, were American. It was simply that he was convinced the United States had designs on Canada, that it would seek enormous influence in Canada if only because it feared the prospect of an attack across the North Pole. It was simply that he was a genuine Canadian nationalist in the Laurier mould who believed that the best policy was for Canada to be left alone and to leave alone. Involvement meant trouble and trouble meant strain on national unity, something to be avoided at all costs. As the postwar policies to which the Department of External Affairs generally subscribed come under increasing scrutiny, King's position may not appear as ignominious as some have supposed.

The relationship between the aspirations of the officers of External Affairs and genuine fears of Soviet power is, of course, an important and difficult one. That the necessity to contain revolutionary Communist ideology was real for many Canadian officials is obvious enough. Escott Reid, a senior Department officer in the years after the war, wrote that "We saw the tide of Russian power moving across Europe."[27] and Georges Vanier, the Ambassador to France told Mackenzie King in September, 1948 that "the

Russians are really barbarians. They would take all of the individuals [in France] who are of the elite, educated, carry them off to Russia and make them work in the mines, the rest of the population becoming slaves of Russian conquerors."[28] Mackenzie King himself needed little convincing that World War III was just around the corner.

One wonders just how much American sources of information contributed to Canadian perceptions on this score. If, as some revisionists contend, American leaders like Truman and Acheson were building upon wartime suspicions of Russia and exaggerating the menace in statements to Congress and the public, then perhaps Canadian officials were manipulated as well.[29] One good example of this kind of process is the account printed in the Pearson memoirs of a briefing from Secretary of State Acheson after the outbreak of war in Korea. The war, Acheson told Pearson, was only "a phase, and not, in the long run, the most important phase, of the general conflict between the free and the communist worlds." Korea itself was relatively unimportant, but the challenge "must be met by the free peoples; that they must call a halt to communist aggressive tactics." Most important, as Pearson recorded, "Mr. Acheson emphasized, and more than once, that the most significant deduction to be made from the Korean attack was the necessity for strengthening as rapidly as possible the forces of the free world to meet aggression elsewhere." The Korean incident underlined the dangers of the international situation

and in doing so had made it politically possible for the United States to secure congressional and public support for a quick and great increase in defence expenditures; for further assistance to those of its friends who are willing to make a similar increased effort.... The naked aggression of the communists ... had made this possible, and ... the USSR has made a great and stupid mistake in permitting, and possibly encouraging, this aggression.

The main thing, Acheson argued after making his pitch for a Canadian contribution to the war, "was for the free democracies to work together to strengthen their defences and their war economies immediately."[30] Clearly the United States was using the Korean War to obtain broad support for policies of American and European rearmament; equally clear, the Canadian government would take the same tack. Whether Pearson was seduced by Acheson's rhetoric, however, is doubtful; he seemed to need precious little convincing.

Yet not all Canadian officials shared the prevailing view. Dana Wilgress, Ambassador in Moscow during and just after the war, was remarkably non-alarmist in his assessments of Soviet intentions,[31] and John Holmes, the Chargé in Moscow in early 1948, reported that "the USSR does not want to provoke a shooting-war until they have exhausted all their other tactics." Another Moscow Embassy despatch observed that "few people in the world are more apprehensive of an imminent war than those about us.[32] General Maurice Pope, the Canadian representative in Berlin, was particularly skeptical of the frightened reactions in Ottawa and Washington. Even during the Berlin blockade, Pope did not see any Soviet intentions for a general advance, though he was convinced that Russia had the power to do so.[33] Moreover, the General was convinced that the belligerency of the Americans was equally to be feared. When on 5 April, 1948 word came that Soviet fighters had shot down a British aircraft, Pope mused that "it is a godsend that it was a British and not an American civil aircraft that had suffered, for if it had been otherwise, many of us in the British sector felt, Lucius Clay [the American representative], with his characteristic energy, would have filled the air with American fighters to spill all Russia military aircraft out of the skies.''[34] In the East Block, however, the doubts about American policy and Soviet intentions seem usually to have been put aside.

If the sources of and reasons for Ottawa's perceptions of the Russians need further research with recent revisionist questions in mind, so too does the relationship between Canadian foreign policy activism and the general public. There are always difficulties in assessing public opinion either through the press, articles, or polls. How much do public sentiments reflect official manipulation, for example? What is the impact in Canada of American media? On the surface, at least, it appears that the Canadian public moved with its government to international activism far more easily than did the American people. Certainly this was true insofar as Parliament is concerned, for there was general agreement in the House of Commons on the British loan, on NATO and on Canadian contributions to the UN force in Korea.

Were any scare tactics of a kind employed by Acheson and Truman used on the Canadian people? Every Canadian leader had to consider national unity, the perennial Canadian problem in a time of international crisis. This was not misplaced concern, of course, for no politician who had lived through the harrowing conscription debates of 1942 and 1944 could forget it. Thus it is not too much to suppose that Prime Minister St. Laurent and his colleagues found congenial a line of argument about an expansive Communist conspiracy which held promise of a positive response in Quebec. The Church had repeatedly condemned Communism, and Soviet repression of Catholicism in Eastern Europe was not calculated to win approval along the shores of the St. Lawrence. Even then, however, Quebec opinion lagged behind the rest of the country on foreign policy issues, and thus continued attention was required.[35]

The government, committed to internationalism and determined to show support for the general contours of United States policy, was prepared to cultivate a positive public response. In a speech to a Richelieu Club meeting shortly after he became Prime Minister, for example, St. Laurent turned to a bishop at the head table and pointedly said, "Your Excellency, we would not like to see you stand the type of trial which Cardinal Mindszenty had to undergo."[36] His remarks in the House of Commons in support of the North Atlantic Treaty in March, 1949 were also aimed at the *Québecois*: the communists opposed Canada's joining NATO

> to permit the expansion of that ideology of Communist and atheistic terrorism. I know that in my province, among the people of my race and religion, there is no wish that disasters such as those which have come to so many European countries should be repeated here, and that the situation within former democratic countries of Europe which has given rise to religious persecution which has shocked the whole civilized world should come to pass in Canada.[37]

At the same time, it must be remembered that for many Canadians no such tactics were necessary. One might have expected some skepticism from the CCF, but very little seems to have existed. "Contrary to the propaganda against the proposed North Atlantic Treaty," M. J. Coldwell claimed, "the proposal is not an attempt on the part of so-called American imperialism to bring western European democracies into an alliance for the purpose of destroying the Soviet Union. It originates in the anxiety of western European democracies to persuade North America to support them in a defensive union."[38]

The relationships among economic imperatives, political ideology, and public opinion in the formation of Canadian foreign policy during the early Cold War years are by no means clear at this point; the precise role U.S. pressures might have had in shaping the outcomes also requires investigation. What can be said with some certainty, however, is that whatever its domestic sources, Canadian policy necessarily interacted with U.S. goals in the postwar world. And so any change in our perception of the latter forces a reconsideration of the former. A reassessment of U.S. initiatives forces us to take another look at the Canadian response.

And the obverse is true. A reconsideration of Canadian policy can have significant implications for the current American revisionist critique. The dual perspective provided by even so tentative a reading of both Canadian and American histories as this forces us to the conclusion that if American policy in the Cold War years was neither so uniquely misguided nor self-interested as many U.S. critics suggest, Canadian policy was far less virtuous than its champions are prepared to admit.

CHAPTER EIGHT

CANADA AND THE PERILS OF "EXEMPTIONALISM"

During his visit to Ottawa in Spring, 1972 President Richard Nixon explained the implications of the Nixon Doctrine for Canada to a joint session of the Houses of Parliament. "That doctrine rests on the premise that mature partners must have autonomous independent policies." It recognizes "that we have very separate identities; that we have significant differences; and that nobody's interests are furthered when these realities are obscured." It follows that "each nation must define the nature of its own interests; each nation must decide the requirements of its own security; each nation must determine the path of its own progress."[1]

While Canadians might feel pleased by this affirmation of Canadian autonomy by a U.S. President, they cannot afford to contemplate the future of Canadian-American relations with easy optimism. As several commentators noted at the time, in acknowledging Canada's right to pursue her self-interest the President also claimed the same prerogative for the United States.[2] This means in fact that the Nixon Doctrine heralds a major turning point in the future of Canadian-American relations because it challenges one of the most enduring aspects of Canadian-

151

American relations in the past: the Canadian habit of seeking exemptions from American economic regulations in order to avoid the costs of national independence. Canada had done this fairly successfully in 1917 with the IMB-Ordnance Department agreement. Mackenzie King had done it again in 1941.

The same kind of policy seemed to make good sense in the postwar years, for accepting the overall direction of United States policy as Canada's own national guidelines did not seem an excessively high political price to pay. In the current climate of growing nationalism, however, the regular treks by Canadian negotiators southward have an aura less of opportunity than of subservience. The habit has not changed; but opinion about its significance has. The debate over the importance of the ten percent surcharge, DISC legislation, and other aspects of recent United States economic policy should, if nothing else, stimulate consideration of the roots of Canadian-American economic relations.

If the present tension over national economic questions alerts us to a longstanding feature of Canadian-American relations, it also alerts us to the crucial role that war crises have played in their development. Periods of war historically have been especially important sources of American emergency regulations and of subsequent Canadian exemptions. No modern country has fought a major war without economic controls, notwithstanding the American hope of avoiding them with Vietnam. The wage and price controls and other economic measures, including the surcharge, comprise a belated recognition of the hard realities of war in the twentieth century. As Harold Innis pointed out many years ago, many American economic regulations are, *de facto*, North-American regulations,[3] and every major conflict, from the Great War to Vietnam, has both accelerated Canadian involvement in United States economic regulations and also underscored Canada's habit of embracing the general outlines of even discriminatory American economic policy while seeking to gain exemptions for herself.

Pointing to historical forces over which they had no real influence has been one of the traditional defences of Canadian policy-makers. What happened had to happen; an historical offense is the best defence. Constraints on Canadian policy-making cannot be ignored, of course. As Jon McLin notes in his study of Canadian defence policy: "to focus upon Canada raises the danger, which always exists in writing about lesser powers, of exaggerating the extent to which Canada's policies result from its national decisions, rather than from external factors over which it has little or no control."[4] It is always true in a certain sense that the politics of colonial countries are defined elsewhere. It is almost a cliché now to point out that at least from Confederation onward the mere existence of a dynamic, expansive society to the south has precipitated a series of defensive moves by the Canadian state.

But it is not historically accurate to leave the matter there, for to do so would be to overlook two factors: first, the way in which Canadian decision-makers have had their own self-interest to serve in responding to American initiatives; and second, how on the specific, day-to-day level, Canadian élites have had a share in shaping the nature of Canadian-American relations. More specifically, because they believed it enhanced their prestige, power, and economic opportunity, they have accepted American policy in general while seeking special concessions for themselves. Canadian diplomats, for example, encouraged the United States on the road to globalism after World War II in part to fulfill their sometime hope of becoming the linchpin between Europe and the United States. Canadian economic and political élites have sought exemptions from

United States economic regulations in times of crisis in order to maintain a corporate capitalist society at home and to gain some influence abroad. They have served their own particular domestic purposes even while the consequences of their actions, whether intended or not, have supported American global diplomacy abroad. Let us look at this syndrome once again through a re-examination of Canadian-American economic relations during World Wars I and II.

The Great War, a watershed in so much of world history, was an equally important event in Canadian-American relations. On the very broadest level, the war signalled the beginning of the end of Britain as a world power and the transformation of the United States from a debtor to a creditor nation. "The United States," Mackenzie King predicted on 4 August, 1914, "will rise out of the situation as the first power of the world. . . . The British Empire will be changed in complexion, the mother country will be crushed by the burden of the war."[5]

The specific implications for Canada of this tranformation could only be seen dimly in 1914, but as the war dragged on and British financial resources contracted, Canada was forced to turn to the United States for economic assistance. According to the *Monetary Times*, for example, the United States purchased forty-two percent of all Canadian bond issues in 1915, and sixty-five percent in 1916, whereas previously Britain had purchased from fifty to eighty percent.[6] But the United States money market closed when the United States entered the war in April, 1917 and the Wilson Administration soon clamped on credit controls. How Sir Thomas White, Finance Minister in the Borden Government coped with this fact is interesting for at least two reasons. Not only did White set an important precedent in the development of exemptionalism, but he did so in a way that illustrates how Canadian officials tried to reconcile the hopes for independence with the realities of economic interdependence. White argued successfully with Treasury Secretary William McAdoo that Canada should be exempt for at least the amount of its adverse trade balance with the United States. But rather than accept a direct loan from the United States Government he chose to enter the New York money market, even at the cost of an appreciably higher interest rate. "We shall have to pay a fairly stiff rate of interest," explained White, "but I believe I would rather do this than borrow directly from the Government of the United States even at a lower rate of interest. In other words, I would rather we should 'hoe our own road'."[7] Canada continued to obtain preferential treatment in American money markets throughout the war. "This is something," boasted the *Monetary Times*, "of which Canada can very well feel proud."[8]

American entry into the war posed additional challenges to the Canadian economy, for over half of the coal and iron ore for the Dominion's booming munitions industry came from the United States. Warnings had been raised earlier about potential United States shortages, but nothing systematic was done to expand Canadian coal and steel industries in the meantime, and the North American scramble for war materials intensified throughout the summer and fall of 1917. The Canadian Fuel Administration was established in the summer of 1917 to procure United States supplies, and Canadian representatives travelled to Washington that fall to lobby for steel requirements.

There is no evidence that the Borden Government used Canada's control over electrical power supplies at Niagara Falls as a bargaining tool with the United States. Federal-provincial conflicts would have reduced its effectiveness in any case, but more importantly Canadian manufacturers were anxious not to antagonize their American suppliers by hard bargaining. "Canada must have coal," warned the *Financial Post*. "We cannot afford to prejudice our case by repudiating power contracts."[9] In the face of financial problems and a consequent decline in British munitions orders placed in Canada in late 1917, together with an increase in orders to the United States, the Government began to push hard for a share of the United States defence market. By September, 1918, J. W. Flavelle's Imperial Munitions Board and the Canadian War Mission had secured eighty-four million dollars worth of American ordnance contracts.[10]

Canada conducted herself much like a regional lobby seeking favors in wartime Washington after April, 1917; and sensitivity to the wishes and needs of American officials followed as a matter of course. "The Canadian Government will have to make a strong presentation of their case [for coal supplies] which I think a perfectly proper one," explained the head of the Canadian War Mission. "A long list of exemptions has been made . . . but I think it will be necessary to follow the wishes of [the] Government here as far as possible without interfering with necessary war work."[11]

In negotiating for favors, Canada played on her dependency relationship and also underscored the contribution her productive capacity could make and had already made to the general Allied cause. Canadian officials, aided by British representatives, used both points with good effect to gain exemptions from two important U.S. decisions: that all foreign purchases must pass through a centralized Allied Purchasing Commission; and that any United States loans to the Allies must be spent in the United States. Not only were Canadian buyers permitted to compete for U.S. supplies on an equal footing with their American counterparts, but Treasury officials ultimately allowed the Allies to spend U.S. loans on Canadian purchases. This was the positive side of Canada's role as a regional lobby group, of her inability to compete for American resources as a distinct nation state in company with the other Allies.[12] A headline in the *Financial Post* in 1917 summed up the consequences: "Canada's Prosperity to Depend on Close Cooperation in Aims and Objects with the United States."[13]

The nationalism and self-confidence so often noted in Canada's experience during the Great War was grounded in a war-induced prosperity inextricably linked to Canada's special place in a Washington-centered economic framework. This relationship was not institutionalized, however. After all, Canada was still very much a part of the British Empire in 1918. Yet the experience left an important legacy. The lobbying activity of the Canadian War Mission was the forerunner of permanent diplomatic representation in Washington and an important stimulus to north-south trade flows. And Great Britain's obvious if understandable inability to protect and guarantee Canadian economic interests in the war enhanced the attractiveness of special deals with the United States. But above all, the war experience was the beginning of a policy of U.S. exemptions in the short-run in lieu of a long-run strategy for Canadian industrial development. It is ironic, of course, that Sir Robert Borden and his colleagues who had fought reciprocity in 1911 should try so hard to encourage the free flow into Canada of materials and contracts from the United States.

While the basic pattern of exemptionalism was set during World War I, it was formalized and encased in bureaucratic machinery only during World War II. The key step in this process was the Hyde Park Declaration of 20 April, 1941 which set out guidelines for American purchases of defence articles. This agreement was designed to solve Canada's adverse trade balance with the United States, which had come about through a sharp rise in imports of capital equipment, raw materials, and components for war production. Canada drew roughly thirty percent of the material for her munitions output from the United States. Under normal circumstances these purchases might have been covered by Canadian dollar surpluses with the United Kingdom, but by the end of 1940 Britain was unable any longer to pay U.S. dollars for her war orders.[14] The United Kingdom's shortage of American dollars had already begun to threaten U.S. munitions production and brought about the decision for Lend-Lease which authorized President Roosevelt to transfer material to any country whose defence was considered vital to United States security.

Although Canada certainly qualified for the kind of Lend-Lease aid awarded Britain and the other Allies, the King government preferred to substitute a policy of direct, large-scale U.S. munitions purchases. The response was not unlike Sir Thomas White's decision to use private bankers rather than the United States Treasury. "Ottawa apparently believed that it is well to keep Canada as independent as possible," commented one sympathetic observer, "and to avoid borrowing or begging as long as may be."[15] But as one student of wartime cooperation has quipped, "The precise form which any loss of independence entailed in lend-lease assistance might have taken is far from obvious."[16] The emotional implications, of course, were clear enough.

More likely is the calculation by Canadian officials that a share of the United States defence market along the lines followed in the First World War would guarantee Canadian access to U.S. machine tools, fuel supplies, and the other elements of war production; and that economic coordination and cooperation on a North-American scale would minimize dislocation in Canada after the war. A jungle of boards and committees arose to coordinate the production of specific items. Canada became part of the United States system of priorities; it set up a Washington mission; the U.S. War Production Board, in turn, established a headquarters in Ottawa. The volume of sales to the United States mounted from $275 million in 1942 to $301 million in 1943 and $314 million in 1944. It then declined to $189 million in 1945.[17]

The experience of 1939-1945 differed in another way from the First World War in that the crisis generated by armed conflict did not cease at war's end and political élites in both the United States and Canada continued to mobilize their peoples for activist foreign policies. The Cold War very quickly ruled out a retreat into isolationism. It also guaranteed that the pattern of exemptionalism, born during war emergencies, would become institutionalized as a permanent part of Canadian-American relations in the post-war years. The immediate issue was nothing less than Canadian prosperity; and the preferred solution was European purchases in Canada financed by American credits.

While American leaders prepared their public to accept the extension of United States global power, Canadian officials searched for the means to their elusive goal of sharing in an American-based prosperity without losing their political independence. The practical issue on which these larger considerations turned once again was the country's balance of payments problems with the United States. In order to stimulate British buying, the government advanced a $1.25 billion loan in 1946 with conditions similar to a $3.75 billion loan later advanced by the United States, but neither was sufficient to pump economic life into a prostrate England. By the end of 1947 Canada faced a severe "dollar crisis," and in November the government set up controls and restrictions to conserve U.S. dollars. The government banned the import of certain items, including washing machines, radios, jewellery, set quotas for textiles and toys, and imposed excise taxes on automobiles. Although this program avoided a devaluation of the dollar, it did not stimulate European buying, nor did it guarantee Canadian prosperity.[18]

It was the Marshall Plan, proclaimed by President Truman in April, 1948 that pulled Canada out of an impasse. More particularly, it was the United States decision to permit the recipients of its aid to make Canadian purchases. By the terms of the ultimate agreement, supplies needed in Europe which could not be purchased in the United States could be bought in Canada with U.S. funds. It seems likely that Canadian promises to lift the recent restrictions on U.S. imports were made. But in any case, the purpose of the bargaining was to gain Canada a place within the protective framework of American financial might. "When we consider what the alternatives would have been," commented one sympathetic analyst in 1948, "Canadians have every reason to welcome the [Marshall] Programme and to cooperate in its execution."[19] By April, 1949, $706 million worth of Marshall Plan credits had found their way to Canada, enough to help pull Canada through her exchange crisis."[20]

The United States has since granted Canada a whole series of exemptions, though their impact may have been less dramatic than the exemption on Marshall aid expenditures. In the five years between 1963 and 1968, for example, the Kennedy and Johnson Administrations introduced a series of measures to fight the United States' growing balance of payment problems. Three of the proposals — the Interest Equalization Tax of July, 1963, the Voluntary Cooperation Program of December, 1965,

and the Mandatory Direct Investment Guidelines of
January, 1968 — applied to Canada; all would have
restricted access to American capital; all resulted in
delegations to Washington; and all produced Canadian
exemptions.

One of the deeper ironies of modern Canadian history is
that the triumph of Canada's past strategy of
exemptionalism has been so great as to endanger her
political future. Though obscured during periods of
emergency and war crises, this fact has emerged with
alarming clarity in recent years, in part because of the
coming end of the Cold War and the beginnings in Canada
of a more realistic assessment of the goals of American
financial power. While in each case Canadian officials may
have believed that the kinds of exemptions they
chose — private instead of public loans, or direct purchases
instead of lend-lease, for example — helped to guarantee
independence, the historical consequences have proven to
be just the opposite. Exemptionalism has offered only an
illusion of independence while it bound the country ever
more firmly into lockstep with American policy.

The United States has not responded to Canadian pleas
out of benevolence, of course, though that factor cannot
be wholly discounted, at least for the war years. Canada
has had bargaining points, and from an American point of
view the presence of an ever-increasing number of branch
plants has added a certain logic to the Canadian approach.
Moreover, it has been a long-standing hope of U.S. policy
to forge an American system in the Western hemisphere
which would encompass Canada, Mexico and the rest of
Latin America. After interviewing Adolf Berle, one of
Franklin Roosevelt's economic advisors, in June, 1940,
Bruce Hutchison concluded: "His studies relate to the new
American Empire. I can describe it as nothing else. He has
been working, he said, on the re-organization of the

economy of all North and South America to make it independent of the world."[21]

But on a more practical level, one of the central facts of exemptionalism in the past has been its relatively small political and economic costs to the United States. During the Great War, for example, some American congressmen wondered why coal should go to Canada when shortages existed at home. But official reassurances and Canadian demonstrations of sacrifice deflated a potential political issue. In his study of Canadian-American economic relations during World War II, Warren James observed on this point that "Canada's needs from the United States were usually relatively small and did not materially influence levels of consumption in the United States." But he warned, more prophetically than he realized, that while "there was never any very serious controversy over exports to Canada, ... under less favorable conditions, it is probable that public pressures would have forced a much more vigorous scrutiny of the freehand extension of the principles of economic cooperation laid down in the Hyde Park Declaration."[22]

This brings us to the present, and to the essence of the Nixon Doctrine. Exemptions are no longer going to be so easy for Canada to come by because the Vietnam war is the one recent war which has not strengthened the American economy. On the contrary, it has plunged it into crisis. In the wake of the United States' own economic and social problems it is the limits and not the opportunities of the American system which have come into focus. The Nixon Doctrine promises that when the United States institutes tough measures in her own self-interest Canada will have to fend for herself.

The source of the present "time of troubles," however, by no means derives exclusively from American policy. The Canadian present has been shaped by the Canadian past. In the current atmosphere of nationalism, with its search for a mythic history, there is a danger that the domestic impulse behind Canada's place in the American system will be overlooked. Even though a critical eye on the Canadian past is in order, close attention to current shifts in U.S. policy is obviously of the essence too. For just as American initiatives interacted with Canadian responses to define Canadian-American relations in the past, the same dialectic will shape them in the future. It is highly likely, moreover, if there are any lessons in history, that policy initiatives will continue to come from the United States. And it is highly likely, again if the past is any guide, that only an American refusal to grant exemptions in the future will move Canadian political and economic élites from a policy of exemptionalism to a policy of independence.

APPENDIX

THE HYDE PARK DECLARATION

Among other important matters, the President and the Prime Minister discussed measures by which the most prompt and effective utilization might be made of the productive facilities of North America for the purpose both of local and hemisphere defence and of the assistance which in addition to their own programme both Canada and the United States are rendering to Great Britain and the other democracies.

It was agreed as a general principle that in mobilizing the resources of this continent each country should provide the other with the defense articles which it is best able to produce, and, above all, produce quickly, and that production programmes should be coordinated to this end.

While Canada has expanded its productive capacity manyfold since the beginning of the war, there are still numerous defense articles which it must obtain in the United States, and purchases of this character by Canada will be even greater in the coming year than in the past. On the other hand, there is existing and potential capacity in Canada for the speedy production of certain kinds of munitions, strategic materials, aluminum and ships, which are urgently required by the United States for its own purposes.

While exact estimates cannot yet be made, it is hoped that during the next twelve months Canada can supply the United States with between $200,000,000 and $300,000,000 worth of such defense articles. This is a small fraction of the total defense programme of the United States, but many of the articles to be provided are of vital importance. In addition, it is of great importance to the economic and financial relations between the two countries that payment by the United States for these supplies will materially assist Canada in meeting part of the cost of Canadian defense purchases in the United States.

In so far as Canadian defense purchases in the United States consist of component parts to be used in equipment and munitions which Canada is producing for Great Britain, it was also agreed that Great Britain will obtain these parts under the lease-lend act and forward them to Canada for inclusion in the finished articles.

The technical and financial details will be worked out as soon as possible in accordance with the general principles which have been agreed upon between the President and the Prime Minister.

(External Affairs Records, file 1497-40, Tel. 62, Secretary of State for External Affairs to Secretary of State for Dominion Affairs, London, 22 April, 1941.) (This file is retained in the Department).

NOTES

Chapter One
Organizing for War:
Canada and the United States during World War I

1. Mao Tse-Tung, *Selected Writings*, Peking, 1963, p. 228.

2. Hans Speier, *Social Order and the Risks of War*, Cambridge, Mass., 1964, p. 261. See Quincy Wright, *A Study of War*, Chicago, 1942, for a remarkably comprehensive compilation of data on war.

3. For a theoretical discussion of the distinction drawn here between "state" and "society," see Randall Collins, "A Comparative Approach to Political Sociology," in Reinhard Bendix (ed.), *State and Society, A Reader in Comparative Political Sociology*, Boston, 1968, pp. 48-50.

4. All the statements made in this paragraph could be illustrated many times over by events in either Canada or the United States during World War 1. The state smashed antiwar groups like the I.W.W., but many trade groups and industries gained strength, while still other organizations like the Canadian National Dairy Council, or the Union Party for that matter, came into being for the first time. The work of organizational zealots can be studied in the formation of National Research Councils in both countries, and the Council of National Defense and the Advisory Commission in the United States. Engineers and psychologists in the United States offer good examples of groups seeking to increase their public prestige through the war effort. Psychology had "helped win the war," concluded Robert M. Yerkes, a former president of the American Psychological

Association who introduced personnel testing to the army in the war. "At the same time, it has incidentally established itself among the other sciences and demonstrated its right to serious reconsideration in ... human engineering," (cited in Daniel J. Kevies, "Testing the Army's Intelligence: Psychologists and the Military in World War I," *Journal of American History*, 54, 1968, pp. 565-81). The relationship between the extension of state regulation and planning and the formation of interest groups is explored by Harry Eckstein, in Harry Eckstein and David E. Apter, eds., *Comparative Politics*, New York, 1963, pp. 389-97. See also William Preston, *Aliens and Dissenters*, Cambridge, 1963; Michael R. Johnson, "The I.W.W. and Wilsonian Democracy," *Science and Society*, 28, 1964, pp. 257-74; *Canadian Annual Review 1918*, p. 507; Grosvenor B. Clarkson, *Industrial America in the World War, The Strategy Behind the Line, 1917-1918*, Boston, 1923, ch. II; Helen Wright, *Explorer of the Universe, A Biography of George Ellery Hale*, New York, 1966, ch. 14; Mel Thistle, *The Inner Ring, The Early History of the National Research Council of Canada*, Toronto, 1966, chs. 1, 2; Samuel Haber, *Efficiency and Uplift*, Chicago, 1964, ch. VII.

5. Stanislaw Andrzejewski argues that the greater the proportion of the total population used in military purposes the greater the democratizing effects of the war. See his *Military Organization and Society*, London, 1954, esp. ch. II.

6. J. A. Corry, "The Growth of Government Activities in Canada, 1914-1921," *Canadian Historical Association, Report 1940*, pp. 63-73. The best recent survey of Canada's organizational efforts in the war is R.C. Brown and Ramsay Cook, *Canada 1896-1921: A Nation Transformed*, Toronto, 1974, chapters XI-XII.

7. Corry, pp. 63-73.

8. There is no comprehensive account available on the origins and administrative history of the Council of National Defense. See, however, the *First Annual Report ...* , *of the Council of National Defense during the World War*, Document No. 193, 73rd Cong., 2nd Sess., Washington, 1934.

9. Henry Borden, ed., *Robert Laird Borden: His Memoirs*, New York, 1938, II, p. 686.

10. David Carnegie, *The History of Munitions Supply in Canada*, London, 1925, pp. 29, 33, 47, chs. X and XXIV.

11. *Canadian Annual Review 1917*, pp. 363-7.

12. Raymond Aron, *The Century of Total War*, New York, 1954, p. 87.

13. In an essay on "the garrison state," written in 1941, Harold Lasswell distinguished between the specialist on bargaining, who is the businessman, and the specialist on violence, who is the soldier. In 1914, the businessman was more powerful in society than the soldier in the United States, but the trend of the times, felt Lasswell in 1941, was toward the supremacy of the soldier and a merging of skills, "starting from the traditional accoutrements of the professional soldier, moving toward the manager and promoter of large-scale civilian enterprise," Harold D. Lasswell, "The Garrison State," *American Journal of Sociology*, 46, 1941, pp. 455-68.

14. This quotation is cited in Frank Freidel, *Franklin D. Roosevelt, The Apprenticeship*, Boston, 1952, pp. 288-9. See also Joseph L. Morrison, *Josephus Daniels, The Small-d Democrat*, Chapel Hill, 1966; and Jerold S. Auerbach, "Woodrow Wilson's Prediction to Frank Cobb: Words Historians Should Doubt Ever Got Spoken," *Journal of American History*, 54, 1967, p. 612.

15. There are many references in the secondary literature to Wilson's concerted campaign to win businessmen to his Administration after 1914. See Arthur S. Link, *Woodrow Wilson and the Progressive Era, 1910-1917*, New York, 1963, pp. 75-80, 228-9; and *Wilson: The New Freedom*, Princeton, 1956, pp. 446-57, 469-71; and Robert H. Wiebe, *Businessmen and Reform: A Study of the Progressive Movement*, Cambridge, 1962, pp. 141-2.

16. Manuscript Division, Library of Congress, Woodrow Wilson Papers, Wilson to Kenneth McKellar (Dem., Tenn.), 9 July, 1917.

17. *Canadian Annual Review 1918*, p. 431.

18. For an example of such an approach on the American side, see K. Austin Kerr, "Decision For Federal Control: Wilson, McAdoo, and the Railroads, 1917," *Journal of American History*, 54, 1967, pp. 550-60, and "American Railroad Politics, 1914-1920," Ph.D. dissertation, University of Pittsburgh, 1965. Kerr views the origins and operations of the Railroad Administration in the context of economic and political conflicts prevalent in the railroad industry in the prewar years.

19. Quoted in Allen F. Davis, *Spearheads for Reform, The Social Settlements and the Progressive Movement, 1890-1914*, New York, 1967, p. 222.

20. *Ibid.*, p. 226. For an elaboration of the achievements of welfare reform during the war see Allen F. Davis, "Welfare, Reform and World War I," *American Quarterly*, 14, 1967, pp. 516-33.

21. *Canadian Annual Review 1917*, p. 312. Fred Davis Baldwin

discusses the American Army's efforts in this direction in "The Enlisted Man in World War I," unpublished Ph.D. dissertation, Princeton University, 1964. Canadian and American historians have generally neglected the social history of the war years. We would do well to follow the example of British historians and sociologists like Arthur Marwick and Richard Titmuss who have tried to deal with the relationship between war and social change in Britain: Arthur Marwick, *The Deluge: British Society and the First World War*, London, 1965; *Britain in the Century of Total War, War, Peace and Social Change 1900-1967*, Boston, 1968; and "The Impact of the First World War on Britain," *Journal of Contemporary History*, 1968; Richard M. Titmuss, "War and Social Policy," in his *Essays on "The Welfare State*," London, 1958, pp. 75-87.

22. The following brief description of the WIB is based on research in the primary sources and on a reading of such secondary treatments as Grosvenor B. Clarkson, *Industrial America*; Robert F. Wilson, *The Giant Hand: Our Mobilization and Control of Industry and Natural Resources, 1917-1918*, Vol. I of *How America Went to War*, New Haven, 1921; Daniel R. Beaver, *Newton D. Baker and the American War Effort, 1917-1919*, Lincoln, 1966; Paul A. C. Koistinen, "'The Industrial-Military Complex in Historical Perspective: World War I," *Business History Review*, 41, 1967, pp. 378-403; Robert D. Cuff. "A 'Dollar-a-Year-Man' in Government: George N. Peek and the War Industries Board," *ibid.*, pp. 404-20; "The Dollar-A-Year Men of the Great War," *The Princeton University Chronicle*, 30, 1968, pp. 10-24; and "Bernard Baruch: Symbol and Myth in Industrial Mobilization," *Business History Review*, 43, 1969, pp. 385-407.

23. Richard H. Hippelheuser, ed., *American Industry in the War, A Report of the War Industries Board* (March 1921), New York, 1941, p. 21.

24. Yale University Library, Edward M. House Papers, Lovett to House, 22 December, 1917.

25. U.S. Congress, Senate, Committee on Military Affairs, *Investigation of the War Department, Hearings* . . . 65th Cong., 2nd Sess. Washington, 1918, pt. 3, p. 1863.

26. Wilson Papers, Daniel Willard to Wilson, 7 December, 1917.

27. For an illustration of these points in a secondary source, see Louis Galambos, *Competition and Cooperation: The Emergence of a National Trade Association*, Baltimore, 1966, pp. 65-6.

28. Lewis H. Haney, "Price Fixing in the United States during

the War (pt) III," *Political Science Quarterly*, 34, 1919, p. 446.

29. Federal Records Center (Suitland, Mo.), Records of the War Industries Board, Minutes of the Price Fixing Committee of the War Industries Board, vol. 5, "Meeting of the . . . Committee with Representatives of the Hide and Leather Industry. . . ." 19 July, 1918. Cited hereafter as Mins. P.F.C.

30. Princeton University Library, Bernard M. Baruch Papers, "Statement of A. W. Shaw."

31. Mins. P.F.C., vol. 4, "Meeting of the Price Fixing Committee . . . . with special Committee Representing the Cotton Fabrics Industry . . ." 29 May, 1918.

32. Records of War Industries Board, Box 178, file 21B-A5, Baruch to Guggenheim, 16 June, 1918.

33. For an amplification of this point see James Weinstein, *The Corporate Ideal in the Liberal State*, Boston, 1968, ch. 8.

34. Canadian industrialists like A. T. Drummond, president of Canada Sugar Refining Co. Ltd. and T. H. Wardleworth, president of the National Drug and Chemical Company, encouraged the Canadian government to cooperate with the universities to foster industrial research, an idea enthusiastically received by Principal W. Peterson of McGill and President R. A. Falconer of the University of Toronto. Professor J. C. McLennan of the Department of Physics at Toronto was particularly active as a liaison between industry and the universities. The Minister of Trade and Commerce wrote McLennan about an Advisory Council to coordinate university research in May, 1916: "My idea is to have seven or nine on the Board, and to have two of these representative of the industrial interests — and five scientific men, men versed in industrial research work. We want men of science, of course, but we also want men of a practical turn who have business in them." Foster had his Council approved, 6 June, 1916, and the members (of the National Research Council) were named 29 November, 1916. Mel Thistle, *The Inner Ring*, ch. 1, esp. pp. 4, 6-8. See also the *Canadian Annual Review 1916*, p. 445; *1917*, pp. 469-70. 35. William E. Leuchtenburg, *The Perils of Prosperity, 1914-1932*, Chicago, 1958, pp. 41-2; and "The New Deal and the Analogue of War," in John Braeman, *et al.*, eds., *Change and Continuity in Twentieth Century America*, Columbus, Ohio, 1964; Gilbert C. Fite, *George N. Peek and the Fight for Farm Parity*, Norman, 1954; Albert U. Romasco, *The Poverty of Abundance, Hoover, the Nation, the Depression*, New York, 1965, pp. 109-12, 119, 151, 162-6.

Chapter Two
Symbol of a Relationship:
The Ordnance Department-IMB Agreement of 1917

1. Public Archives of Canada, Sir W. T. White Papers, Vol. 8, Flavelle to Borden, 7 November, 1917.

2. *Ibid.*

3. P.A.C. J. W. Flavelle Papers, Vol. 23, Col. Jay E. Hoffer (Ordnance Department) to IMB, 20 December, 1917.

4. U.S. Senate, 74th Cong., 2nd Sess., Special Committee on Investigation of the Munitions Industry, *Munitions Industry*, Report No. 944, Washington, 1946, Part 6, p. 148; Cleona Lewis, *America's Stake in International Investments*, Washington, 1938, pp. 119, 352; Milton Friedman and Anna Jacobson Schwartz, *A Monetary History of the United States 1867-1960*, Princeton, 1963, p. 199; E. V. Morgan, *Studies In British Financial Policy, 1914-1952*, London, 1952, p. 309; and R. H. Brand, *War and National Finance*, London, 1921, pp. vii-xii.

5. Morgan, *Studies In British Financial Policy, pp. 355-6.*

6. For background on the Anglo-French loan see *Munitions Industry*, Report No. 944, Ch. 2; Richard W. Van Alstyne, "Private American Loans to the Allies, 1914-1916," *Pacific Historical Review*, 2, 1933, pp. 180-93; and Thomas W. Lamont, *Across World Frontiers*, New York, 1950, pp. 67-8.

7. Morgan, *Studies In British Financial Policy*, pp. 324-5.

8. *Documents on Canadian External Relations (DCER)*, Ottawa, 1967, I, p. 60, Prime Minister to Acting High Commissioner in United Kingdom, 26 November, 1914. The increasing British difficulties can be seen in the telegrams exchanged between Ottawa and London in 1914-1915, P.A.C., Department of Finance Records, Vol. 596, file 155-40.

9. *DCER* I, pp. 80, 81, 83, 84, Acting High Commissioner to Prime Minister, 6 July, 1915; Colonial Secretary to Governor General, 6 July, 1915; Acting High Commissioner to Prime Minister, 10 July, 1915; Minister of Finance to Acting High Commissioner, 22 July, 1915.

10. *DCER* I, p. 91, Acting High Commissioner to Prime Minister, 23 October, 1915.

11. Flavelle Papers, Vol. 24, quoted in Flavelle to R. H. Brand, 4 August, 1916.

12. *DCER* I, p. 130, Governor General to Colonial Secretary, 5

August, 1916.

13. White Papers, Vol. 8, White to Flavelle, 7 November, 1916.

14. On the $50 million loan of 1917, see Department of Finance Records, Vol. 596, File 155-38-3; on the $75 million loan to the IMB in 1917, see *ibid.*, File 155-38-2.

15. See the following surveys of Canadian war finance: Sir Thomas White, *The Story of Canada's War Finance*, Montreal, 1921; J. J. Deutsch, "War Finance and the Canadian Economy, 1914-1920," *Canadian Journal of Economics and Political Science*, 6, 1940, pp. 525-37; F. A. Knox, "Canadian War Finance and the Balance of Payments, 1914-18," *ibid.*, pp. 226-57; and R. Craig McIvor, *Canadian Monetary, Banking and Fiscal Development* Toronto, 1958, Ch. 6. All of these surveys assume an inevitability about the development of Canadian war finance which does a serious injustice to the particular dynamics of its emergence. They are, in effect, less historical than they could be.

16. White Papers, Vol. 8, Flavelle to White, 15 December, 1916.

17. Quoted in David Lloyd George, *War Memoirs*, 6 vols., London, 1933, III, p. 1713.

18. William Gibbs McAdoo, *Crowded Years*, Boston and New York, 1931, p. 375.

19. Lloyd George, *War Memoirs*, III, p. 1699.

20. McAdoo's drive for power as an administrator was well known in Washington, as were his presidential ambitions. His colleague, Secretary of War Newton D. Baker, claimed McAdoo had "the greatest lust for power I ever saw." From "Interview with M. Newton D. Baker ..." in Library of Congress, Washington, D.C., Papers of Ray S. Baker, Box 20; on this point see also Arthur S. Link, *Wilson: The New Freedom*, Princeton, 1956, p. 115. On Anglo-American economic rivalry see Carl P. Parrini, *Heir to Empire, United States Economic Diplomacy, 1916-1923*, Pittsburgh, 1969.

21. Quoted in Sir Arthur Willert, *The Road To Safety: A Study in Anglo-American Relations*, London, 1952, p. 116.

22. The best and most recent analysis of the loan issue is W. B. Fowler, *British-American Relations 1917-1918, The Role of Sir William Wiseman*, Princeton, 1969, Ch. 3. See also McAdoo, *Crowded Years*, pp. 392-3, 396, 399, 401, 412; Willert, *The Road to Safety*, pp. 116-19; Lloyd George, *Memoirs*, III, pp. 1700-01, 1714-15, 1718; and H. Montogomery Hyde, *Lord Reading*, New York, 1967, pp. 210-12.

23. Queen's University, Flavelle Papers, Box 4, White to Flavelle,

13 June, 1917, enclosed cable British Consul-General, New York, to Governor General, 12 June, 1917.

24. *DCER* I, p. 170, Colonial Secretary to Governor General, 30 June, 1917.

25. *Ibid.*, p. 171, Lloyd George to Borden, 5 July, 1917.

26. *Ibid.*, pp. 171-2, 174, 176, 177, 179, 187-8, Governor General to Colonial Secretary, 7, 17, 20 July, 1917, 20 August, 1917, and 5 September, 1917; Colonial Secretary, to Governor General, 10 August, 1917; and Minister of Finance to High Commissioner, 20 December, 1917. See also White's memorandum, 3 September, 1917, recapitulating events and listing the Canadian concessions. Department of Finance Records, Vol. 761, file 304-1A-1. Sir Thomas White made a postwar defence of his actions during the summer crisis in a letter to the Toronto *Globe*, 10 March, 1927.

27. *DCER*, I, p. 176, Governor General to Colonial Secretary, 20 July, 1917. For additional examples of Canadian pressure on this point, see White to High Commissioner, 14 May, 1917; and Flavelle to Minister of Munitions, 6 July, 1917, both in Department of Finance Records, Vol. 761, File 304-1A-1. The government also arranged for the chartered banks to loan the U.K. $100 million for wheat purchases "upon the condition that the Treasury obtain $250,000,000 from sources outside of Canada." The outside source was the U.S., of course, and the Canadians were warned to make "no mention . . . of fact that United States Treasury has promised finance Canadian crops." *Ibid.*, file 155-35-14, "Memorandum of Agreement . . . 31 October, 1917," and tel. Reading to White, 12 October, 1917.

28. National Archives, Washington, D.C., U.S. Treasury Department, Bureau of Accounts, Record Group 39, "Country File," Canada, Box 24, list enclosed with White to McAdoo, 21 June, 1917. According to Urquhart and Buckley, the Canadian trade deficit with the U.S. was in 1914: $139,316,000; 1915: $135,873,000; 1916: $343,770,000; 1917: $422,016,000. M. Urquhart and K. Buckley, eds., *Historical Statistics of Canada*, Toronto, 1965, p. 183.

29. *DCER* I, p. 172, Borden to Lloyd George, 7 July, 1917. But of course the British had their own difficulties in New York. "I am afraid question of our utilizing credits received from Government of the United States for Canadian payments is quite impracticable," the Chancellor of the Exchequer wired White, at one point. "We should

not have pressed you so strongly if we had had any hope of relief from that quarter." Department of Finance Records, Vol. 761, file 304-1A-1, Chancellor of the Exchequer to White, 9, July, 1917.

30. *DCER* I, p. 172, Borden to Lloyd George, 7 July, 1917.

31. *Financial Post*, 1 September, 1917, p. 1. In early August, the *Post* had reported "that there have been no important contracts placed for several months, and that final orders are now being filled by a number of firms." *Ibid.*, 11 August, 1917, p. 1. On the same point see also *ibid.*, p. 18, 25 August, 1917, p. 1. For references to cutbacks in farm products as well see *ibid.*, 8 September, 1917, p. 1.

32. Flavelle Papers, Vol. 24, Flavelle to R. H. Brand, 7 August, 1917.

33. In mid-October, 1917, Flavelle informed C. B. Gordon, vice-chairman of the British War Mission in Washington: "There has been a great deal of activity among Canadian manufacturers who either have gone to the United States to solicit business, or have been solicited by people in the United States to sell their plants. These have included cartridge case people, the Energite Loading Plant at Renfrew, forging plants at Kingston, at Galt and at Hamilton. It has included shrapnel plants where the manufacturer has no prospect of orders from us." *Ibid.*, Vol. 34, Flavelle to Gordon, 17 October, 1917. The Steel Company of Canada was among those who pressed the IMB for reasons why it should not sell its munitions facilities. It finally sold its forgings plant in September, 1918. See William Kilbourn, *The Elements Combined: A History of the Steel Company of Canada*, Toronto and Vancouver, 1960, p. 106.

34. Flavelle Papers, Vol. 24, Flavelle to Brand, 14, 21 August, 1917; "Draft of Telegram to Ministry of Munitions," 17 August, 1917; Vol. 34, Flavelle to Gordon, 10 September, 1917 and 23 October, 1917.

35. For Flavelle's opinions and activities concerning American defence contracts in Canada see Flavelle Papers, Vol. 22, Flavelle to W. O. Hugard, 3 August, 1916; Vol. 24, Flavelle to Brand, 15 April, 1916, 9 October, 1917, and 6 November, 1917; Vol. 34, Flavelle to Gordon, 17 and 23 October, 1917. In the autumn of 1917 Canada had an unused capacity for shell-forging and machining of 200,000 to 250,000 shells per week. David Carnegie, *The History of Munitions Supply in Canada*, London, 1925, p. 217. The *Financial Post* reported the arrival of Canada's first U.S. war orders (for textiles) in early July, and it urged an extension of the trend in

subsequent reports. See *Financial Post*, 7 July, 1917, p. 1; 4 August, 1917, p. 1; 15 September, 1917, p. 1.

36. RG 39, Bureau of Accounts, Box 24, White to McAdoo, 21 June, 1917.

37. *Ibid.*, Thomas W. Lamont to McAdoo, 26 June, 1917.

38. For the details of the negotiations of June-July, see *ibid.*, Assistant Secretary of the Treasury to Sir Cecil Spring-Rice, 13 July, 1917; and "Secretary McAdoo Said . . ." (notes of a conference with White), 25 July, 1917, *ibid.*; as well as White Papers, Vol. 4, F. W. Taylor to White, 24 July, 1917 and White to Taylor, 26 July, 1917; Borden Diary, 19 July, 1917; and *Financial Post*, 4, 21, 28 July, 1917, pp. 1, 12.

39. Hyde, *Lord Reading*, p. 217; Fowler, *British-American Relations*, pp. 57-8. There are only indirect references to Reading's efforts on behalf of Canada in the secondary accounts.

40. Flavelle Papers, Vol. 24, Brand to Flavelle, 5 October, 1917. The fullest account of the negotiations is in Carnegie, *History of Munition Supply in Canada*, pp. 219ff.

41. Flavelle Papers, Vol. 24, Flavelle to Brand, 9 October, 1917.

42. *Ibid.*, Vol. 34, Gordon to Flavelle, 16 October, 1917.

43. For references to the Washington talks of IMB and Mission representatives see *ibid.*, Flavelle to Gordon, 17 October, 1916; Vol. 26, Gordon to IMB, 18 October, 1917; Vol. 54, Minutes of the Imperial Munitions Board, Minute Book No. 1, 18 October, 1917 and 1 November, 1917.

44. *Ibid.*, Vol. 34, Flavelle to Gordon, 17 October, 1917.

45. Quoted in White Papers, Vol. 3, Flavelle to Borden, 7 November, 1917.

46. *Financial Post*, 3 November, 1917, pp. 1, 8. For an appreciative, though more restrained, business opinion, see "Financing Our Foreign Trade," *Monetary Times*, 59, 16 November, 1917, p. 9.

47. P.A.C., Robert Borden Papers, Vol. 238, Borden to Flavelle, 18 April, 1918.

48. *Ibid.*, Flavelle to Borden, 16 April, 1918.

49. (Queen's) Flavelle Papers, Box 4, Flavelle to W. E. Rundle, 7 May, 1918.

50. *Ibid.* See also P.A.C., Flavelle Papers, Vol. 54, Minutes of the IMB, Minute Book No. 1, 2 May, 1918, for another reference to the $56 million figure. Flavelle indicated later to Sir Robert Borden that the value added for steel and components should be fifty to seventy

percent. Borden Papers, Vol. 238, 26 August, 1918.

51. Flavelle Papers, Vol. 25, Flavelle to Brand, 11 June, 1918.

52. White Papers, Vol. 9, Flavelle to White, 25 September, 1918; and Borden Papers, Vol. 246, Flavelle to Borden, 4 September, 1918. British orders in Canada through the IMB declined steadily from the summer of 1917. Payments fell from $43,956,000 in July, to $23,042,000 in March. See "Payments Made In Canada By Imperial Munitions Board Year Ending March 31st, 1918," 10 June, 1918, enclosed with J. H. Gundy to Flavelle, 20 June, 1918, (Queen's) Flavelle Papers, Box 4. "Our operations, as you know," Flavelle observed in March, 1918, "are much smaller than they wery six months ago." Flavelle to E. R. Wood, 5 March, 1918, *ibid.*, Box 5.

53. *Report of Chairman of Imperial Munitions Board to the Minister of Munitions*, 17 August, 1921, appendix I in Carnegie, *History of Munitions Supply In Canada 1914-1918*, p. 303. Carnegie's 1925 study, however, puts the total inflow into Canada at $50,855,575.97, with a further $28,837,671.06 awarded in claims settlements. *Ibid.*, p. 226.

54. Henry Borden, ed., *Robert Laird Borden: His Memoirs*, New York, 1938, II, p. 769.

55. *Ibid.*, pp. 772-3.

56. Flavelle Papers, Vol. 35, Memorandum, Flavelle to Lloyd Harris, 9 August, 1918.

57. *Ibid.*, Flavelle to Harris, 10 December, 1917.

58. *Ibid.*, Vol. 23, Flavelle to Borden, 10 May, 1918. For the background on an additional price differential between Canadian and American orders see Carnegie, *History of Munitions Supply in Canada 1914-1918*, pp. 221-2.

59. Flavelle Papers, Vol. 35, F. A. Rolph (of the Canadian War Mission) to Flavelle, 26 April, 1918.

60. *Ibid.*, Harris to Flavelle, 1 May, 1918.

61. Borden Papers, Vol. 244, Flavelle to Harris, 25 October, 1918; Flavelle to Borden, 25 October, 1918; Vol. 238, Harris to Flavelle, 24 October, 1918. American contractors were also caught at the war's end with outstanding claims against the War Department, many of them also of dubious legal standing. Businessmen in such emergency agencies as the War Industries Board lobbied for Congressional legislation to guarantee these informal agreements. See Robert D. Cuff, *The War Industries Board, Business — Government Relations during World War I*, Baltimore and London, 1973, pp. 261-2.

62. Flavelle Papers, Vol. 35, Flavelle to L. Harris, 7 October, 1919. But see Carnegie, *History of Munitions Supply in Canada 1914-1918*, pp. 225-6 for a more happy assessment.

63. Some U.S. officials wondered if perhaps Canadians gained unjustifiable advantages in these arrangements. For an example of skepticism in the Treasury Department, see [George O. May] "Memorandum for Mr. Leffingwell," 6 August, 1918, in RG 39, Bureau of Accounts, Box 24.

64. *Ibid.*, White to McAdoo, 2 June, 1918.

Chapter Three
Lloyd Harris and the
Canadian War Mission to Washington

1. For a very general survey of the diverse British Missions see W. G. Lyddon, *British War Missions to the United Stattes, 1914-1918*, London, 1938. Borden's determination to have Canadian representatives attached to the Balfour Mission is evident in Public Archives of Canada, Sir Robert Borden Papers, Borden Diaries, 11 April, 1917; *ibid.*, Vol. 89, Sir George Foster to Borden, 12 April, 1917; Arthur Meighen to Borden, 14 April, 1917; Borden to Foster, 16 April, 1917; Vol. 88, Borden to Foster, 16 April, 1917. See also P.A.C., Sir W. T. White Papers, Foster to W. T. White, Vol. 18, 30 April, 1917.

2. M. Urquhart and K. Buckley, eds., *Historical Statistics of Canada*, Toronto, 1965, p. 169.

3. The British Ambassador, Sir Cecil Spring-Rice, summarized the traditional, prewar patterns of U.S.-Canadian relations in a memorandum. P.A.C., Sir Joseph Pope Papers, Vol. 115, "Notes on the Manner in Which Canadian Business is Transacted in Washington," dated 29 January, 1918. See also, *ibid.*, Spring-Rice to Pope, 31 January, 1918.

4. The fullest description of Wilsonian war government is William F. Willoughby, *Government Organization in War Time and After*, New York, 1919.

5. Pope Papers, Vol. 116, Pope to Borden, 26 May, 1917.

6. *Ibid.*

7. *Ibid.*, Pope to Borden, 24 September, 1917. Documentation for this incident can be found in *ibid.*, Vol. 115. See as well the memorandum prepared for Robert Lovett by Pope and Major G. A. Bell, Assistant to the Minister of Railways, in Federal Records

Center, Suitland, Md., Record Group 61, Records of the War Industries Board, Box 106, File 21A-A4, cited hereafter as RG 61.

8. This summary of Gordon's activities is based upon the documents in P.A.C., Sir Joseph Flavelle Papers, Vol. 34.

9. *Ibid.*, Vol. 24, Flavelle to R. H. Brand, 17 April, 1917.

10. *Ibid.*, Vol. 22, Flavelle to Baruch, 16 and 25 May, 1917; and Vol. 32, Fitzgerald to Flavelle, 28 May, 1917.

11. *Ibid.*, Vol. 54, Minutes of the IMB, 17 May, 1917, Minute Book No. 1.; Vol. 34, Flavelle to Gordon, 19 July, 1917.

12. *Ibid.*, Vol. 24, Brand to Flavelle, 8 September, 1917.

13. *Ibid.*

14. *Ibid.*, Brand to Flavelle, 9 October, 1917.

15. *Ibid.*, Flavelle to Brand, 9 October, 1917; and see also Flavelle to Brand, 15 October, 1917.

16. Borden Papers, Vol. 88, Magrath to Borden, 7 September, 1917.

17. Cited in Robert Bothwell, "Canadian Representation at Washington: A Study in Colonial Responsibility," *Canadian Historical Review*, 53, 1972, p. 135.

18. P.A.C., Department of External Affairs Records, Box 264106, file 996, Governor General to Colonial Secretary, 31 October, 1917.

19. *Ibid.*

20. For a convenient, detailed summary see Bothwell, "Canadian Representation at Washington." See also *Documents on Canadian External Relations*, Ottawa, 1967, I, *1909-1918*, pp. 24 ff

21. Flavelle Papers, Vol. 24, Flavelle to Brand, 15 October, 1917.

22. University of Toronto, Sir Edmund Walker Papers, Box 22, [Manager of the Brantford Canadian Bank of Commerce] to E. Walker, 3 February, 1916.

23. William Kilbourn, *The Elements Combined: A History of the Steel Company of Canada*, Toronto and Vancouver, 1960, pp. 58-62.

24. See the memorandum of a meeting, 1 March, 1911, between Borden and, among others, Harris, printed in Paul Stevens, ed., *The 1911 General Election: A Study in Canadian Politics*, Toronto, 1970, pp. 69-70.

25. *Financial Post*, 20 October, 1917, p. 7. The Russell Motor Car Co. received $17,394,247 worth of contracts from the Shell Committee and IMB with all but $2 million coming from the IMB.

Companies affiliated with Russell Motor Car Co. received over $10 million in contracts. See Queen's University, Sir Joseph Flavelle Papers, Box 5, "Orders Placed By Shell Committee and Imperial Munitions Board," attached to Flavelle to R. H. Brand, 4 March, 1919.

26. P.A.C., Sir George Foster Papers, Diaries, Vol. 6, 30, 31 October; 1, 2 November, 1917; Borden Diaries, 25 October, 5 November, 1917. At one point Flavelle believed Harris might return to politics himself. Flavelle Papers, Vol. 34, Flavelle to C. B. Gordon, 2 August, 1917.

27. *Ibid.*, Vol. 35, Harris to Flavelle, 20 November, 1917.

28. *Ibid.*, Harris to Flavelle, 26 November, 1917.

29. *Ibid.*, Harris to Flavelle, 5 December, 1917.

30. See Flavelle Papers, Vol. 35 for fuller documentation.

31. *Ibid.*, Flavelle to Harris, 10 December, 1917.

32. Borden Diaries, 7 January, 1918.

33. Borden Papers. Vol. 95, Harris to Borden, 19 January, 1918.

34. *Ibid.* See also Henry Borden, ed., *Robert Laird Borden: His Memoirs*, New York, 1938, II, pp. 767-8. In mid-January the War Committee of the Cabinet appointed a special committee of businessmen to examine U.S. war government and report back. This special committee also recommended a Canadian War Mission. See Department of External Affairs Records, Box 265101, File 168, "Extracts from the Minutes of a Meeting of the War Committee . . . January 14, 1918." A similar recommendation came from the Montreal Harbour Commissioners, *ibid.*, Box 265106, File 996, W. G. Ross to C. C. Ballantyne, 14 January, 1918.

35. Borden Papers, Vol. 95, Loring C. Christie, "Memorandum for the Prime Minister," 30 January, 1918.

36. *DCER* I, pp. 32-4.

37. Borden Papers. Vol. 95, Borden to Harris, 1 February, 1918.

38. *Ibid.*, Harris to Borden, 5 February, 1918.

39. Department of External Affairs Records, Box 265101, File 169, 996/18 with the following: L. Harris to A. K. McLean, 28 March, 1918; Borden to Governor General, 13 May, 1918; "Canadian War Mission Washington, D. C. Staff as of 15th May 1918." See also Foster Papers, Vol. 65, J. Pope to A. Meighen, 15 December, 1928; and "Report upon the Canadian Bureau of Information, New York City, and the Canadian War Mission, Washington."

40. Borden Papers, Vol. 95, Wilson to Borden, 22 February, 1918.

41. Flavelle Papers, Vol. 34, Gordon to Flavelle, 24 July, 1917.

42. Borden Papers, Vol. 95, R. Boudreau to Governor General, 30 January, 1918.

43. *Ibid.*, Vol. 95, Jones to Borden, n.d. [January, 1918].

44. Flavelle criticized Canadian steel companies for failing to enlarge their capacities. Flavelle Papers, vol. 23, Flavelle to Borden, 25 January, 1917. Sir George Foster noted the effect of the steel issue on the Commerce Department's work load. See Foster Papers, Diaries, Vol. 6, 22 August, 22 and 28 September, 1917. For the "steel controller" reference see *Financial Post*, 4 October, 1917, p. 1. See also *ibid.* 6 October, 1917, p. 1. For Trade and Commerce appeals to the War Trade Board see Records Center, Suitland, Md., Record Group 182, Records of the War Trade Board, entry 63, Box 361, F. C. T. O'Hara to H. B. Van Sinderin; cited hereafter as RG 182.

45. The War Trade board had already indicated its suspicion to the Commerce Department. See RG 182, entry 63, Box 361, Bureau of Exports to R. T. C. O'Hara, 18 December, 1917. On the role of Harris and the Canadian War Mission see Flavelle Papers, Vol. 11, Harris to Flavelle, 31 January and 1 February, 1918; and RG 61, Box 105, File 21A-A4, Frank A. Rolph to J. L. Replogle, 16 February, 1918.

46. RG 61, box 106, File 21A-A4, E. B. Parker to C. M. Wooley, 11 June, 1918, and related correspondence.

47. RG 182, entry 63, Box 360, McMaster to J. A. Parker, 9 May, 1918.

48. *Ibid.*, Box 359, McMaster to J. A. Parker, 23 October, 1918. For their part, American officials continued to suspect Canadian buyers of taking unfair advantage of their access to cheaper American supplies and never failed to urge Canadians to tighten up their regulatory apparatus. RG 61, Box 106, File 21A-A4, E. B. Parker to J. L. Replogle, 24 October, 1918; and RG 182, entry 63, Box 359, J. A. Parker to R. H. McMaster, 18 October, 1918. Pressure upon the Canadian administrators to coordinate their policies with U.S. regulations is especially evident in the meetings of the War Trade Board. See RG 182, entry 6, Records of the Executive Office: Minutes of meetings of the War Trade Board, 11 December, 1917; 6 and 10 June, 1918; 25 July, 1918.

49. For an elaboration of the complexities of Ontario Hydro see H. V. Nelles. "The Politics of Development," Ph.D. Thesis, University of Toronto, 1970. American officials indicated their concern

about supplies of Ontario hydro-electricity as early as April, 1917. See RG 61, Box 34, File 21A-A3, Brig. Gen. William Crozier (Chief of Ordnance) to Advisory Committee, Council of National Defense, 9 April, 1917; and *ibid.*, Eugene Meyer, Jr., to Frank A. Scott, 21 June, 1917. Drayton's report of October, 1917, is in Borden Papers, Vol. 95.

50. The final report of Robert J. Bulkley, the WIB's power expert, in RG 61, Box 34, File 21A-A3, is attached to Bulkley to E. B. Parker, 9 November, 1917.

51. Borden Papers, Vol. 222, L. L. Summers (the WIB's chemicals chief) to J. Flavelle, 18 January, 1918; and R. J. Bulkley to Borden, 2 March, 1918.

52. Flavelle responded here to a suggestion from the WIB's power expert to close down the British Forgings Toronto plant so as to release power for the American Cyanamid Company and the Union Carbide Company. Borden Papers, Vol. 222, Flavelle to Borden, 6 March, 1918; Bulkley to Borden, 2 March, 1918.

53. *Ibid.*, Harris to Borden, 31 January, 1918.

54. RG 61, Box 105, File 21A-A4, Legge to Parker, 13 February, 1918. Bulkley told Canadian officials the next month that any steel lost from closing the British Forgings plant would be replaced from U.S. sources. Borden Papers, Vol. 222, Bulkley to Borden, 2 March, 1918.

55. *Financial Post*, 24 November, 1917, p. 10; 8 December, 1917, p. 1; and 19 January, 1918, p. 10.

56. Borden Papers, Vol. 222, Rowell to Drayton, 8 March, 1918.

57. *Ibid.*, Harris to Borden, 3 April, 1918. See also *ibid.*, Harris to Borden, 25 April, 1918.

58. *Canadian Annual Review 1918*, p. 553.

Chapter Four
The Hyde Park Declaration, 1941:
Origins and Significance

1. The Agreement is found in Appendix 1.

2. House of Commons *Debates*, 28 April, 1941, p. 2289. See also Louis Rasminsky, "Foreign Exchange Control: Purposes and Methods," in J. F. Parkinson, ed., *Canadian War Economics*, Toronto, 1941, p. 127. For press views on Hyde Park, see Public Archives of Canada, W. L. M. King Papers, ff.C275492 ff.

3. These figures are from Corelli Barnett, *The Collapse of*

British Power, London, 1972, p. 14. In 1943, the Treasury representative in Ottawa valued U.K. holdings of U.S. securities at $950 million on 31 August, 1939; at $616 million on 31 December, 1940; and at $372 million on 3 August, 1941. P.A.C., Department of Finance Records, Vol. 3437, R. G. Munro to W. C. Clark, 5 February, 1943. In 1944, Lord Keynes estimated that total U.K. reserves were $4.2 billion in September, 1938, $2.45 billion in September, 1939 and precisely $12 million (!) in April, 1941. King Papers, Memo, "British Requirements for the first year of Stage II, n.d. [Oct. — Nov., 1944], ff.C251055ff.

4. Cited by David Dilks, "Appeasement Revisited," *University of Leeds Review*, 15, 1972, p. 51.

5. Warren F. Kimball, "Lend-Lease and the Open Door: The Temptation of British Opulence, 1937-1942," *Political Science Quarterly*, 86, 1971, pp. 240-1. See also Warren F. Kimball, *The Most Unsordid Act, Lend-Lease, 1939-1941*, Baltimore, 1969, pp. 64-5, 86-7.

6. R. S. Sayers, *Financial Policy 1939-1945*, London, 1956, pp. 335-6.

7. John M. Blum, *Roosevelt and Morgenthau, A Revision and Condensation of From the Morgenthau Diaries*, Boston, 1970, p. 341.

8. Kimball, "Lend-Lease and the Open Door," p. 258. In this article Kimball makes the distinction between the generally benign motives that guided Morgenthau and the origins and passage of Lend-Lease, and the aggressively economic motives which dominated its subsequent use by Secretary of State Cordell Hull, who shaped the broader economic policies of the Roosevelt Administration.

9. There is a large body of material on this subject. See, for example, Public Record Office, London, Cabinet Records, Cab 65/2, War Cabinet Minutes, 2 December, 1939. For a Canadian view, see King Papers, Notes and Memoranda, vol. 151, folio 1274.

10. See for example M. M. Postan, *British War Production*, London, 1952, p. 229; Queen's University, Norman Rogers Papers, "Record of Visit to the United Kingdom.... 18 April — 9 May, 1940," entry for 19 April, 1940, p. 5; King Papers, Tel. No. 97, King to Churchill, 8 June, 1940, f.250514.

11. Sayers, *Financial Policy*, pp. 328-32, 335.

12. House of Commons *Debates*, 29 April, 1941, p. 2338; King Papers, W. C. Clark to King, 9 April, 1941, ff.288021ff. Clark hoped to persuade the U.S. to allow Canada to get a share of the British

gold. But on gold, cf., Department of Finance, W. C. Clark Papers, file B2-8-9-1, Memo by Clark, "Report on Visit to Washington, March 17-21, 1941."

13. Sayers, *Financial Policy*, p. 338.

14. H. D. Hall, *North American Supply*, London 1955, p. 230. A later and probably somewhat more accurate estimate for fiscal 1941-1942 puts the national income at $5.95 billion. War spending was estimated at $1.45 billion, aid to Britain at $1.15 billion and civil expenditures at $1 billion. The total of public expenditure amounted to $3.6 billion or 60.5 percent of national income. King Papers, "Canada's War Effort," 4 April, 1941, ff.288088ff. See also Clark Papers, file B2-8-9-1, "Canada's War Effort and Budgetary Position," 4 March, 1941, and P.A.C., Ian Mackenzie Papers, file 2-29, Senior to Mackenzie, 28 April, 1941. By comparison, in the Great War the percentage of national income devoted to war at no time rose above ten percent.

15. J. W. Pickersgill, *The Mackenzie King Record*, Vol. 1: *1939-1944*, Toronto, 1960, p. 189; Queen's University, Grant Dexter Papers, Memoranda, 11, 25 March, 1941.

16. Sayers, *Financial Policy*, pp. 322-3.

17. King Papers, Memo, W. C. Clark to King, 9 April, 1941, ff288014ff.; Rasminsky, "Foreign Exchange Control," p. 120. In fact the actual figures were worse even than this estimate.

	Canadian Exports to U.S.	Canadian Imports from U.S.
1938	$270,461,000	$ 424,730,000
1939	380,392,000	496,898,000
1940	442,984,000	744,231,000
1941	559,713,000	1,004,498,000

M. Urquhart and K. Buckley, eds., *Historical Statistics of Canada*, Toronto, 1965, pp. 181-2.

18. House of Commons *Debates*, December 2, 1940, pp. 610-12. See also Clark Papers, file B2-8-9-0 for detail on Canada's exchange situation in late 1940. On U.S. representations over the War Exchange Tax of 1940, see King Papers, Robertson to Skelton, 14 June, 1940, f.C230902.

19. Finance Minister Ilsley summarized these measures in House of Commons *Debates*, 29 April, 1941, pp. 2338-9.

20. J. S. B. Pemberton, ed., "Ogdensburg, Hyde Park and After," *Behind the Headlines*, 1, 1941, p. 18.

21. R. W. James, *Wartime Economic Cooperation*, Toronto, 1949, p. 18. See the good summary, "Canadian Wartime Economic Control Measures," *Bulletin of the Institute of International Finance of New York University*, No. 118, 30 December, 1941.

22. United States National Archives, Washington, State Department Records, 842.00/601, Tel. 322, Moffat to Secretary of State, 24 October, 1940.

23. P.A.C., Department of External Affairs Records, vol. 35, Memorandum, "United States Exchange Discussions," 20 November, 1940.

24. Urquhart and Buckley, p. 168. *The Financial Post* on 1 March, 1941, reported a U.S. Commerce Department estimate of Canadian holdings as $1.18 billion. But W. C. Clark told King that figures reported to the government were only $275 million at 28 February, 1941. King Papers, Clark to King, 9 April, 1941, f.288018. On the Canadian determination to hold on to these U.S. assets, see *ibid.*; Dexter Papers, Memo, 11 March, 1941; P.R.O., Foreign Office Records, FO 371/28795, Phillips to Treasury, 4 March, 1941.

25. King Papers, Clark to King, 9 April, 1941, ff.288023ff. On British pressure, see P.R.O., Treasury Records, T160/1054, "Canadian Financial Assistance to this Country," n.d. [14 March, 1941], att. to MacDonald to Sir Horace Wilson, 17 March, 1941. On U.S. pressure, see Hall, *North American Supply*, pp. 236-7.

26. House of Commons *Debates*, 2 December, 1940, p. 556; King Papers, Robertson to King, 7 April, 1941, ff.287996ff. *The Financial Post*, later reported that Washington had protested the exclusion of fresh fruits and vegetables, hinting at reprisals against Canadian exports. 5 April, 1941, p. 1. These fruit and vegetables amounted to more than twenty percent of total U.S. exports to Canada. Urquhart and Buckley, pp. 180, 182. For the Canadian-American trade agreements of 1935 and 1938, see R. N. Kottman, *Reciprocity and the North Atlantic Triangle 1932-1938*, Ithaca, 1968.

27. For the text of the Lend-Lease Act, see Edward R. Stettinius, Jr., *Lend-Lease, Weapon for Victory*, New York, 1944, pp. 335-9.

28. P.A.C., Privy Council Office, War Cabinet Committee Records, Minutes, 18 February, 1941. Cf. *Financial Post*, 18 January, 1941, p. 1.

29. War Cabinet Committee Records, Minutes, 26 February, 1941.

30. The Secretary of State for Dominion Affairs, Cranborne, sent a long memo to Churchill on this subject in which he criticized the U.S. efforts at hemispheric consolidation which "must ultimately not only poison the relations [between the U.S. and the U.K.] but also drive a wedge between us and Canada." P.R.O., Prime Minister's Office Records, Premier 4/43B/2, 5 March, 1941. Cf. U.K. Treasury Records, T160/1340, L. S. Amery to Kingsley Wood, 10 May, 1941 which indicates that such fears increased after Hyde Park.

31. *Ibid.*, T160/1054, "Canadian Financial Assistance to this Country"; docs. on U.K. Foreign Office Records, FO 371/28791-8; Dexter Papers, Memorandum, 9 April, 1941. This kind of U.K. attitude particularly bothered O. D. Skelton, the Under Secretary of State for External Affairs. As he wrote in a memo of 20 December, 1940, "We should cooperate with the United Kingdom fully and freely in discussions with the United States but we should carry on our own discussions with Washington on these subjects. We have our own angle on the Western Hemisphere and it is Canada that should be laying down the policy in these matters." Memo, "Hemispheric Economic Preparations," in Department of External Affairs, Records, file 1497-40 (Part I). (This file is retained in the Department).

32. Clark estimated that Canada's adverse balance with the U.S. would be $400 million for the year from August 1940 and might be $600 million for the year after that. Canada's remaining capital assets were, in U.S. dollars, $136 millions of gold, $115 millions of dollars, and $378 million in marketable securities. The British Treasury officer observed that if British estimates of their adverse balance with Canada of $1.2 billion were correct it was difficult to see how Canada could carry on. "The proportion of their national income which is required for supplying their war effort . . . is on any showing astonishingly high. . . ." These factors notwithstanding, the Canadians were still opposed to taking Lend-Lease. U.K. Foreign Office Records, FO 371/28792, Phillips to Treasury, 4 February, 1941; FO 371/28795, Phillips to Treasury, 4 March, 1941; James, *Wartime Economic Cooperation*, p. 32; A. F. W. Plumptre, *Mobilizing Canada's Resources for War*, Toronto, 1941, pp. 71ff.; King Papers, C. D. Howe to King, 8 April, 1941, ff.288010ff. But see *ibid.*, Clark to King, 9 April, 1941, ff.288032-3 which defines conditions in which Lend-Lease might be acceptable.

33. Pickersgill, I, p. 189. King was quite right on this point, for the Roosevelt administration under Hull's influence did use Lend-Lease ultimately as a lever to try to break up the Imperial preference

system and to convert Britain to economic multilateralism in the postwar years. See Richard N. Gardner, *Sterling-Dollar Diplomacy*, New York, 1956, pp. 42-56. In analyzing the variety of motives among American postwar planners, E. F. Penrose observed that some Washington officials "were jealous on political grounds of any ties between Canada and Great Britain that were not shared by the United States." E. F. Penrose, *Economic Planning for the Peace*, Princeton, 1953, p. 27. Norman Robertson, in King Papers, Robertson to King, 7 April, 1941, ff.287996ff., seemed to feel that tariff adjustments might help Canada solve some of its exchange problems with the U.S.

34. For a report indicating critical U.S. opinion, see War Cabinet Committee Records, Minutes, 11 February, 1941. For the question of French gold, see U.K. Treasury Records, docs. on T160/1045; U.K. Prime Minister's Office Records, Premier 4/43A/16, J. Garner to J. M. Martin, 15 August, 1940; Pickersgill, I, pp. 180-7.

35. King Papers, Robertson to King, 12 March, 1941, ff.C250323ff. and Clark to King, 9 April, 1941, f.288026. The Viscose sale was the result of a personal request Roosevelt made to Churchill for a spectacular indication of British good faith to appease Congressional opponents of Lend-Lease. See Kimball, *Most Unsordid Act*, pp. 224-5. *The Financial Post*, 29 March, 1941, p. 12, noted the symbolic nature of the event. The briefing papers Clark took to Washington are in Clark Papers, file B2-8-9-1. See particularly his "Report" on the visit for some British opinion on the forced sale of their holdings.

36. War Cabinet Committee Records, Minutes, 12, 13 March, 1941. See on this point, two memos in the King Papers, Brockington to King, n.d., f.C250301, and Robertson to King, 12 March, 1941, ff.C250324-5. The Canadian members of the Permanent Joint Board on Defence had suggested cooperation between Canada and the U.S. in the field of war materials and the integration of production facilities as early as December, 1940. These proposals had already been canvassed in the Washington bureaucracy. U.S. State Department Records, 842.20 Defense/61, Memo, Hickerson to Welles, 21 December, 1940; the memos by H. L. Keenleyside in External Affairs Records, vol. 67, file 383; Skelton's memo to King in *ibid.*, vol. 826, file 725, 23 December, 1940; and material on *ibid.*, file 1497-40 (Part I).

37. Dexter Papers, Memo, 5 March, 1941.

38. Hall, *North American Supply*, pp. 236-7; War Cabinet

Committee Records, Minutes, 21 March, 1941.

39. *Ibid.*

40. Dexter Papers, Memos, 9, 18 April, 1941.

41. War Cabinet Committee Records, Minutes, 12, 13 March, 1941.

42. *Ibid.*, 27 March, 1941; Sayers, *Financial Policy*, p. 339.

43. War Cabinet Committee Records, Minutes, 21 March, 1941. Cf. Clark Papers, file B2-8-9-1, Clark's "Report on Visit to Washington." There is no evidence to suggest that the Americans were interested in forcing the British to buy only in the United States as a condition of Lend-Lease aid. But clearly such a condition would not have been completely unreasonable, and this might have weighed on the minds of Canadian planners.

44. F. D. Roosevelt Library, Hyde Park, Roosevelt Papers, PSF-1, Diplomatic Correspondence — Canada, MacLeish to Roosevelt, 15 February, 1941.

45. L. B. Pearson, *Mike: The Memoirs of the Right Honourable Lester B. Pearson*, Vol. 1: *1897-1948*, Toronto, 1972, p. 226.

46. Pickersgill, I, pp. 190-1.

47. *Ibid.*, p. 190. On the arrangements for the visit and for briefing papers, etc., see King Papers, Black Binders, vol. 409, file 107. The military for example, were concerned with Newfoundland and Canada's place in the U.K. and U.S. military talks. *Ibid.*, ff.287973A-5, f.287976, ff.287991-2.

48. Pickersgill, I, p. 190. King and Hull also discussed the proposed integration of Canadian and American defence production, formally suggested by Canada on March 17. U.S. State Department Records, 842.20 Defense/71, Memo by A. A. Berle, 17 March, 1941. For Hull's version of his talks with King, see Library of Congress, Washington, Cordell Hull Papers, Box 57, folder 196, Memos, 17 April, 1941; for the Canadian Legation's, see External Affairs Records, file 91-CY-40C, H. Wrong to Robertson, 25 April, 1941. (This file is retained in the Department).

49. Hull had wanted the British to put up collateral for Lend-Lease. Cordell Hull, *The Memoirs of Cordell Hull*, 2 vols., London, 1948, II, p. 923. But of his cordiality to Canada there could be no doubt. "Throughout my twelve years at the State Department," he wrote, "no sector of our foreign policy gave me more satisfaction or brought more fruitful results than our relations with Canada." *Ibid.*, p. 1479.

50. Pickersgill, I, pp. 190-2; External Affairs Records, vol. 93,

file 573 (vol. 3), N. Robertson to King, 18 April, 1941; *ibid.* file 91-CY-40-C, Wrong to Robertson, 25 April, 1941. See Clark Papers, file B2-8-9-1, "Memorandum of Meeting with Morgenthau, April 18, 1941" for Clark's meeting with the Secretary. The memo indicates that Morgenthau passed King's suggestion on to the President who liked it.

51. Pickersgill, I, pp. 193-4. According to Wrong, he, Clark and J. C. Coyne of the Legation staff had drafted the statement. External Affairs Records, file 91-CY-40C, Wrong to Robertson, 25 April, 1941.

52. Pickersgill, I, p. 197.

53. *Ibid.*, pp. 198-202; War Cabinet Committee Records, Minutes, 21 April, 1941; Dexter Papers, Memo, 21 April, 1941. Some U.S. officials were distinctly unhappy with the procedures used to negotiate the agreement. See Harvard University, J. Pierrepont Moffat Papers, vol. 19, Hickerson to Moffat, 30 April, 1941.

54. Pickersgill, I, p. 202. Cf. King Papers, Howe to King, 25 April, 1941, ff. 288034Aff. for Howe's detailed response to the terms of the declaration.

55. Press and public could scarcely believe this was so. There was much speculation that Canada had agreed to repeal its ten percent special war tax on imports and the ban on pleasure travel to the U.S. *The Financial Post*, 26 April 1941, p. 1. *The New York Times*, 21 April, 1941, p. 1, groping for a Canadian concession, speculated that the U.S. had secured "a word to say about the form Canadian efforts to aid Britain would take." Rumours were squelched by Isley in Parliament. House of Commons *Debates*, 29 April, 1941, pp. 2339-40. See also Roosevelt Papers, PSF, Canada 1-41, King to Roosevelt, 24 April, 1941; U.S. State Department Records, 842.20 Defense/71, Desp. 1380, Moffat to Secretary of State, 25 April, 1941.

56. C. P. Stacey, *Arms, Men and Governments: The War Policies of Canada 1939-1945*, Ottawa, 1970, p. 490.

57. Memo, 14 May, 1941 on U.S. State Department Records, 740.0011 European War 1939/11542.

58. *Ibid.*, Morgenthau to Hopkins, 15 May, 1941; U.K. Treasury Records, T160/1335, Tel. PURSA Savings No. 2, British Supply Council in North America to Supply Committee, London, 26 July, 1941 and atts. The difficulties should not be underestimated. See External Affairs Records, file 91-CY-40C, Wrong to Robertson, 25

April, 1941; Clark Papers, file B2-8-9-1, Memoranda re Conference in Washington, 11-16 May, 1941.

59. See on this, P.A.C., C. D. Howe Papers, file S-5(91); Hall, *North American Supply*, pp. 237ff.; U.K. Treasury Records, T160/1340, Tel. 1662, High Commissioner, Ottawa, to Dominions Office, 27 October, 1941; U.K. Prime Minister's Office Records, Premier 4/44/9, W.M. (42), 3rd conclusion, item 4; 4th conclusion, item 8; *ibid.*, W.P. (42)14, 7 June, 1942; U.K. Cabinet Records, Cab 65/25, W.C. 3(42), pp. 11-12.

60. J. de N. Kennedy, *History of the Department of Munitions and Supply* 2 vols., Ottawa, 1950, I, p. 475; James, *Wartime Economic Cooperation*, pp. 34-5. James seems to doubt the $200 million figure for orders by mid-1941. *Ibid.*, pp. 35, 193-4. See also Clark Papers, file B2-8-9-1, Memoranda re Conference in Washington, 25-31 December, 1941, which downplays the results of Hyde Park in 1941. The effect of the declaration on 1942 exchange problems, however, was seen to be great although other difficulties remained. For further detail see External Affairs Records, vol. 1009, file 35, "Forecasts of Canada's U.S. Dollar Position," 9 March, 1942, and February, 1943.

61. James, *Wartime Economic Cooperation*, pp. 35-6. Fully $689 million in Canadian securities were purchased by U.S. investors between 1942 and 1945. See W. T. G. Hackett, "The 'Bank,' The 'Fund,' and the Canadian Dollar," in J. D. Gibson, ed., *Canada's Economy in a Changing World*, Toronto, 1948, pp. 119-20; C. D. Blyth, "Some Aspects of Canada's International Financial Relations," *CJEPS*, 12, 1946, pp. 303-4.

62. *The Financial Post*, 1 February, 1941, p. 1.

63. S. D. Pierce and A. F. W. Plumptre, "Canada's Relations with Wartime Agencies in Washington," *CJEPS*, 11, 1945, p. 411. "The agreement," commented W. C. Clark, " . . . represents the fruition of long years of the application of friendliness, goodwill, and common sense to the international relations of the two countries." W. C. Clark, "From the Canadian Point of View," in Reginald G. Trotter and Albert B. Corey, eds., *Conference on Canadian-American Affairs*, Toronto, 1941, p. 86. Cf. the comment by A. A. Berle in a memorandum to Secretary of State Hull: "My own view is that we have a special relation to Canada; and that Canadian defense comes so close to our own that we have to consider Canadian needs as though they were to a considerable extent the needs of the American armed forces." U.S. State Department Records, 842.20

Defense/71, 28 February, 1941. For a very much more qualified view of the continental relationship, see King Papers, N. A. Robertson to King, 22 December, 1941, ff.C161568ff.

64. Urquhart and Buckley, p. 169.

65. Dexter Papers, Memo, 21 April, 1941. King was following Clark's advice in taking this tack. See Clark Papers, file B2-8-9-1, Clark's "Report on Visit to Washington, March 17-21, 1941": King should base "his arguments upon the larger considerations and the more intangible factors in the long term relations between our two countries." Roosevelt also knew how to please his courtiers: "Sometimes I indulge myself in the thoroughly sanctimonious and pharisaical thought, which I hope you are also occasionally guilty of, that it is a grand and glorious thing for Canada and the United States to have the team of Mackenzie and Roosevelt at the helm in days like these. Probably both nations could get along without us, but I think we may be pardoned for our thoughts, especially in view of the fact that our association has brought some proven benefits to both nations." Roosevelt Papers, PSF I, Diplomatic Correspondence — Canada, Roosevelt to King, 5 November, 1941.

66. House of Commons *Debates*, 28 April, 1941, p. 2289.

Chapter Five
Getting on with the Americans:
Canadian Perceptions of the United States, 1939-1945

1. C. P. Stacey, *Arms, Men and Governments*, Ottawa, 1970, esp. chapter 4.

2. Public Archives of Canada, W.L.M. King Papers, "Memorandum to the Minister on Conversations held in Washington . . . 26 January, 1938," ff. C112708ff.; F. D. Roosevelt Library, Hyde Park, Roosevelt Papers, PSF State Dept., S. Welles to FDR, 20 December, 1937; *ibid.*, PSF Welles, Welles to FDR, 10 January, 1938 and January, 1938; Directorate of History, National Defence Headquarters, 000.4 (D14), Memo, Gen. Anderson to Minister of National Defence, 23 November, 1938.

3. (United States Information Service), *Canadian-American Relations 1867-1967*, Ottawa, 1967, III, p. 34.

4. Roosevelt Papers, PPF 3396, FDR to Tweedsmuir, 31 August, 1938.

5. E.g., King Papers, Loring Christie to King, 23 February, 1940, ff. 241080ff.

6. See Stephen Leacock, *All Right Mr. Roosevelt*, Toronto, 1939. Even more foolish was a speech by Gordon Conant, Ontario Attorney-General. See *Toronto Star*, 4 April, 1940; King Papers, Christie to Secretary of State for External Affairs, 4, 11 April, 1940, ff. 241188, 241233-4. For a British response to Conant, see Public Record Office, London, Foreign Office Records, FO 800/398, Campbell to Lothian, 8 April, 1940, and FO 371/25224, Cavendish-Bentinck to Garner, 11 April, 1940.

7. King Papers, Black Binders, vol. 19, I, Memo, by Keenleyside, 29 May, 1940.

8. *Ibid.*, III, Memo by Keenleyside, 23 May, 1940.

9. J. W. Pickersgill, *The Mackenzie King Record*, Vol. I: *1939-1944*, Toronto, 1960, 117ff. The message is on pp. 120-1.

10. King Papers, Black Binders, vol. 19, III, Secretary of State for Dominion Affairs to Secretary of State for External Affairs, 5 June, 1940.

11. Queen's University, Grant Dexter Papers, Memorandum, 7 June, 1940. The memo goes on: "Which indicated Ralston's position fairly well. Willie may be doing all he says but, in any event, he sure has J. L. buffaloed."

12. Library of Congress, Washington, Cordell Hull Papers, folder 194, Memo of Conversation with Canadian Chargé, 17 June, 1940; U.S. National Archives, Washington, State Department Records, 740.0011 Eur War 1939/4700, Memo by A. A. Berle, 12 July, 1940.

13. King Papers, Black Binders, vol. 20, file 77, Typed Diary Note, 13 July, 1940.

14. Copy in University of British Columbia, Alan Plaunt Papers, Box 9, file 1. Among the group were Brooke Claxton, M. P., John Baldwin of the CIIA, Frank Scott of McGill law faculty, Sen. Norman Lambert and others. See *ibid.*, Box 8, file 20, Plaunt to Baldwin, 13 August, 1940. We are indebted to William R. Young for allowing us to use his notes from this collection.

15. King Papers, Towers to King, 15 August, 1940, ff. 25269ff.

16. *Ibid.*, Black Binders, vol. 19, Memorandum, 12 June, 1940.

17. P.A.C., Department of External Affairs Records, vol. 781, file 394, "An Outline Synopsis for a Reconsideration of Canadian External Policy with particular reference to the United States," 17 June, 1940.

18. *Canadian-American Relations 1867-1967*, II, p. 3.

19. See J. L. Granatstein, "The Conservative Party and the Ogdensburg Agreement," *International Journal*, 22, 1966-7, and

James Eayrs, "The Road From Ogdensburg," *Canadian Forum*, 50, 1971, pp. 364 ff.

20. For press response, see King Papers, Notes and Memoranda, vol. 139 and *ibid.*, Christie to Secretary of State for External Affairs, 10 September, 1940, ff. 241378ff.

21. *Ibid.*, Black Binders, vol. 20, file 77, Message of 22 August, 1940.

22. On the PJBD, see C. P. Stacey, "The Canadian-American Permanent Joint Board of Defence," *International Journal*, 9, 1954.

23. See documents on file 1497-40, part I, at the Department of External Affairs, Ottawa. See also, External Affairs Records, vol. 780, file 383 and vol. 826, file 725; State Department Records, 842.20 Defense/71, Memo by A. A. Berle, 17 March, 1941.

24. On Hyde Park, see J. L. Granatstein and R. D. Cuff, "The Hyde Park Declaration of April 1941," *Canadian Historical Review*, 55, 1974.

25. "Pax Americana," *Canadian Forum*, 21, 1941, pp. 69ff. See also the notes on an interview with Berle in External Affairs Records, file 1497-40, 4 February, 1941.

26. The negotiations for the military mission are well handled in Stacey, pp. 354-7. Cf. S. W. Dziuban, *Military Relations Between the United States and Canada 1939-1945*, Washington, 1959, pp. 71ff. See also British documents on this question. Documents on Public Records Office, Dominions Office Records, DO 35/1010 pt. III/WG 476/4/6 and on DO 114/114, pp. 127ff.

27. External Affairs Records, vol. 810, file 614, Memo for the Prime Minister, 22 December, 1941. Cf. memos by Keenleyside in *ibid.*, 27 December, 1941, and 14 April, 1942. For a U.S. appraisal of the new sensitivity in Ottawa, see State Department Records, 711.42/237, "Memo of Conversation with Norman Robertson . . . 19 February 1942." Prof. F. R. Scott characterized the new relationship with Washington as imposing a "dual colonialism" on Canada, adding the U.S. brand to the existing U.K. one. F. R. Scott, "Canadian Nationalism and the War," *Canadian Forum*, 21, 1942, p. 361.

28. P.R.O., Prime Minister's Office Records, Premier 4/44/10, extract from letter, August, 1941.

29. Dominions Office Records, DO 35/1010 A III/WG 476/141, minute, n.d. [early, 1942.]

30. See e.g., King's remarks to the Liberal caucus on 5 June, 1940, in Pickersgill, I, 87.

31. Roosevelt Papers, PSF Canada 1-42, King to FDR, 4 May, 1942.

32. *Ibid.*, PSF-1, Diplomatic correspondence-Canada, Archibald MacLeish to FDR, 15 February, 1941.

33. King Papers, Diary, 20 April, 1940, f. 392.

34. *Ibid.*, 21 March, 1942, f. 251.

35. *Ibid.*, 18 March, 1942 f. 243.

36. Pickersgill, I, pp. 644-5.

37. Vincent Massey, *What's Past is Prologue*, Toronto, 1963, p. 397.

38. But see State Department Records, 711.42/255, Memo, Hickerson to Hull, 20 May, 1943, which indicates real complacency about Canada-U.S. relations.

39. King Papers, "Evidence Relating to United States Efforts . . .", 11 December, 1943 ff. C241909ff.

40. *Ibid.*, "Certain Developments in Canada-United States Relations," 18 March, 1943, ff. C241878ff.

41. External Affairs Records, vol. 110, file 702, Memo for Undersecretary, 29 February, 1944.

42. External Affairs Records, file 7-AD(s), part II, and James Eayrs, *In Defence of Canada*, Vol. III: *Peacemaking and Deterrence*, Toronto, 1972, pp. 320-31, 375-80.

43. Foreign Office Records, FO 371/50365, "Notes on Annual Conference . . ." att. to Holmes to Stephenson, 15 June 1945. For a U.S. view of the same meeting, see State Department Records, 842.00/6-145, Atherton to Secretary of State, 1 June, 1945, and atts.

44. S. D. Pierce and A. F. W. Plumptre, "Canada's Relations with War-Time Agencies in Washington," *Canadian Journal of Economics and Political Science*, 11, 1945, pp. 410-11.

Chapter Six
Corporal Pearson, General Acheson and the Cold War

1. L. B. Pearson, *Mike: The Memoirs of the Right Honourable Lester B. Pearson*, Vol. II: *1948-57*, Toronto, 1973, p. 184.

2. Dean Acheson, *Morning and Noon*, Boston, 1965, pp. 8-12, 25ff.

3. Lester Pearson, *Peace in the Family of Man*, Toronto, 1969, pp. 7-8.

4. Lester Pearson, *Mike: The Memoirs of the Right Honourable*

Lester B. Pearson, Vol. I: *1897-1948*, Toronto, 1972, *passim*.

   5. Acheson, *Morning and Noon*, Chapter 9.

   6. E.g., *Mike* I, p. 30.

   7. Gaddis Smith, *Dean Acheson*, New York, 1972, pp. 423-4.

   8. L. B. Pearson, *Words and Occasions*, Toronto, 1970, p. 72.

   9. *Ibid.*, p. 75. Cf. pp. 82-3.

   10. Quoted in Joyce and Gabriel Kolko, *The Limits of Power*, New York, 1972, p. 650.

   11. L. B. Pearson, *Diplomacy in a Nuclear Age*, Cambridge, Mass., 1959, p. 53. Cf. John Holmes' comment: "The precarious state of the world after 1945 required the forceful intervention in far corners of a benevolent great power like the United States." *The Better Part of Valour*, Toronto, 1970, p. 6.

   12. Pearson, *Words*, p. 34.

   13. *Ibid.*, p. 53.

   14. *Ibid.*, pp. 54-5.

   15. Pearson, *Peace*, p. 10.

   16. *Ibid.*

   17. *Mike* II, p. 22.

   18. Dana Wilgress, *Memoirs*, Toronto, 1967, pp. 144-5. Wilgress changed his mind — he couldn't bear the thought of living in New York.

   19. Smith, *Acheson*, p. 418.

   20. E.g., Dean Acheson, *Grapes From Thorns*, New York, 1972, p. 207.

   21. McGeorge Bundy, ed., *The Pattern of Responsibility*, Boston, 1951, p. 17.

   22. *Ibid.*, pp. 17-18. Gen. Maurice Pope, head of the Canadian military mission in Berlin at the onset of the Cold War, agreed: "I had always felt that my friends, in their search for a mechanism that would ensure international peace and security, had been prone to set their sights too high." *Soldiers and Politicians*, Toronto, 1962, p. 266.

   23. Bundy, *Responsibility*, p. 296

   24. *Mike* I, p. 283.

   25. *Mike* II, pp. 29, 32.

   26. *Ibid.*, pp. 35-6.

   27. *Ibid.*, pp. 25-6.

   28. Escott Reid, "Canadian Foreign Policy, 1967-77: A Second Golden Decade," *International Journal*, 22, 1967, p. 172; See also Arnold Heeney, *The Things That Are Caesar's: Memoirs of a*

Canadian Public Servant, Toronto, 1972, p. 102.

29. Pearson, *Words*, p. 81.

30. *Ibid.*, p. 76; *Mike*, II, p. 44.

31. Pearson, *Peace*, p. 16.

32. See Reid's address of 13 August, 1947, "Canada's Role in the United Nations," Department of External Affairs, *Statements and Speeches*, No. 47/12; the account in F. H. Soward and Edgar McInnis, *Canada and the United Nations*, New York, 1956, pp. 47ff.; and *Mike*, II, p. 40.

33. *Ibid.*, pp. 43, 61ff.

34. *Ibid.*, pp. 55-56. The CCF also made a firm stand on Article 2 the price of its support. House of Commons *Debates*, 28 March, 1949, pp. 2072ff. See also Norman Smith, "Pearson, People and Press," *International Journal*, 29, 1973-4, pp. 9-10, 13.

35. *Mike*, II, p. 56.

36. Dean Acheson, *Present at the Creation*, New York, 1969, p. 277.

37. *Mike* II, p. 57. For Acheson's problems with the Senate Foreign Relations Committee in 1949 see Dean Acheson, *Sketches from Life of Men I Have Known*, New York, 1961, p. 145.

38. *Ibid.*

39. Acheson, *Grapes*, pp. 204-5.

40. *Mike* II, pp. 66-7; Pearson, *Peace*, p. 17; Edgar McInnis, *The Atlantic Triangle and the Cold War*, Toronto, 1959, pp. 36ff.; R. S. Ritchie, *NATO: The Economics of an Alliance*, Toronto, 1956, pp. 3-4 and *passim*.

41. *Mike* II p. 62.

Chapter Seven
Looking Back at the Cold War

1. William Appleman Williams, *The Tragedy of American Diplomacy*, Cleveland, 1959; C. Wright Mills, *The Power Elite*, New York, 1956.

2. Thomas G. Paterson, ed., *Cold War Critics*, Chicago, 1971, *passim*.

3. James T. Patterson, *Mr. Republican: A Biography of Robert A. Taft*, Boston, 1972, p. 435.

4. Eric Sevareid, *Dream, Not So Wild a Dream*, New York, 1946, p. 515.

5. See particularly F. H. Underhill, "Canadian Socialism and

World Politics," from the October, 1950 *Canadian Forum*, a reply to S. W. Bradford, [K. W. McNaught] "The CCF Failure in Foreign Policy," in the previous month's issue. Both are reprinted in J. L. Granatstein and P. Stevens, eds., *Forum: Canadian Life and Letters 1920-70*, Toronto, 1972, pp. 261-6.

6. John Swettenham, *McNaughton*, Vol. III: *1944-1966*, Toronto, 1967, 124; and see also Barton J. Bernstein, ed., *Politics and Policies of the Truman Administration*, Chicago, 1970, *passim*; and Richard Freeland, *The Truman Doctrine and the Origins of McCarthyism*, New York, 1972, *passim*.

7. H. I. Nelson, "Soviet Policy Abroad," *Behind the Headlines*, 7, 1947, p. 24. And see Barton J. Bernstein, "American Foreign Policy and the Origins of the Cold War," in Bernstein, ed., *Politics and Policies of the Truman Administration*, pp. 35-40; and "Cold War Orthodoxy Restated," in *Reviews in American History*, 4, 1973, pp. 453-62.

8. Gabriel Kolko, *Railroads and Regulation, 1877-1916*, Princeton, 1963; *The Triumph of Conservatism, A Reinterpretation of American History, 1900-1916*, Chicago, 1967, esp. pp. 279-305; *The Roots of American Foreign Policy*, Boston, 1969, ch. 1.

9. Joyce and Gabriel Kolko, *The Limits of Power*, New York, 1972, p. 5.

10. *Ibid.*, p. 479.

11. *Ibid.*, pp. 498-9.

12. E.g.s, J. W. Warnock, *Partner to Behemoth*, Toronto, 1970 and Donald Creighton on "Canada and the Cold War," in his *Towards the Discovery of Canada*, Toronto, 1972, pp. 243ff.

13. A good statement of the received version is J. W. Holmes, "Canadian External Policies Since 1945," in his *The Better Part of Valour*, Toronto, 1970, esp. pp. 5-9.

14. Maurice Lamontagne, "Some Political Aspects of Canada's Trade Problem," in J. D. Gibson, ed., *Canada's Economy in a Changing World*, Toronto, 1948, p. 38.

15. House of Commons *Debates*, 16 April, 1946, p. 929.

16. J. W. Pickersgill and D. Forster, eds., *The Mackenzie King Record*, Vol. IV: *1947-8*, Toronto, 1970, p. 125.

17. *Ibid.*

18. Kenneth Wilson, "Dollar Famine," *Behind the Headlines*, 7, 1948, p. 7.

19. See Finance Minister Abbott in House of Commons *Debates*, 22 March, 1949, p. 1788.

20. See Abott in *ibid.* Other opinion-making examples are Wilson, "Dollar Famine," and Lamontagne, "Some Political Aspects."

21. Wilson, "Dollar Famine," p. 9.

22. House of Commons *Debates*, 22 March, 1949, p. 1787; F. L. Rogers, *American Goods in Canadian Markets*, Toronto, 1957, p. 3.

23. F. H. Soward, "Canada in a Two-Power World," *Behind the Headlines*, 8, 1948, p. 22.

24. Lamontagne, p. 21.

25. Pickersgill, IV, p. 135.

26. *Ibid.*, p. 134. See also Denis Stairs, *The Diplomacy of Constraint*, Toronto, 1974, p. 306.

27. Escott Reid, "The Birth of the North Atlantic Alliance," *International Journal*, 22, 1967, p. 434.

28. Pickersgill, 4, p. 391.

29. E.g., see James Eayrs, *In Defence of Canada*, Vol. III: *Peacemaking and Deterrence*, Toronto, 1972, chapter VI.

30. L. B. Pearson, *Mike: The Memoirs of the Right Honourable Lester B. Pearson*, Vol. II: *1948-57*, Toronto, 1972, pp. 149ff. The best study of Canadian policy in the Korean War is Stairs, *Diplomacy of Constraint*.

31. Eayrs, III, pp. 334-5.

32. *Mike*, II, pp. 48-9.

33. M. A. Pope, *Soldiers and Politicians*, Toronto, 1962, p. 338.

34. *Ibid.*, pp. 336, 337, 362. Pickersgill, IV, p. 108 quotes British Prime Minister Attlee sounding very much the same about impatient Americans.

35. See the polling data in J. I. Gow, "Les Québecois, la guerre et la paix, 1945-60," *Canadian Journal of Political Studies*, 3, 1970; J. L. Granatstein, "'Strictly on its Merits': The Conscription Issue in Canada after 1945," *Queen's Quarterly*, 79, 1972.

36. Robert Spencer, *Canada in World Affairs 1946-49*, Toronto, 1959, p. 275.

37. House of Commons *Debates*, 28 March, 1949, pp. 2064-5. Maxime Raymond, leader of the Bloc Populaire Canadien, argued that St. Laurent was using scare tactics on this precise point. *Ibid.*, p. 2683.

38. *Ibid.*, 28 March, 1949, p. 2073.

Chapter Eight
Canada and the Perils of "Exemptionalism"

1. For the text of President Nixon's speech see the *Toronto Star*, 15 April, 1972, p. 11.

2. See, for example, the *Toronto Star*, 17 April, 1972, p. 6; and James Eayrs, "There's a price to pay for our new look in Washington," *ibid*.

3. Mary Q. Innis, ed., *Essays in Canadian Economic History*, Toronto, 1962, p. 239.

4. Jon B. McLin, *Canada's Changing Defense Policy, 1957-1963*, Toronto, 1967, p. 8.

5. Public Archives of Canada, W. L. Mackenzie King Papers, Diary, 4 August, 1914.

6. Fred W. Field, "Retrospect and Prospect," *Monetary Times*, 4 January, 1918, p. 8.

7. P.A.C., Sir W. T. White Papers, Vol. 18, W. Thomas White to George E. Foster, 28 April, 1917.

8. "Financing in United States," *Monetary Times*, 21 December, 1917, p. 9.

9. "Coal and Power Relations," *Financial Post*, 22 December, 1917, p. 10.

10. P.A.C., J. W. Flavelle Papers, Vol. 11, Lloyd Harris to Joseph Flavelle, 26 January, 1918.

11. *Ibid.*

12. The policy debates surrounding these decisions can be followed in National Archives (Washington, D.C.), Records of the Allied Purchasing Commission, 14 November, 1917, 12 February, 1918, 21 March, 1918, 16 May, 1918, all in file 9-A1; and J. C. Carr to British Mission, 6 September, 1918, in file 9-B1.

13. *Financial Post*, 15 December, 1917, p. 1.

14. R. Warren James, *Wartime Economic Co-operation: A Study of Relations between Canada and the United States*, Toronto, 1949, pp. 16-18.

15. A. F. W. Plumptre, *Mobilizing Canada's Resources for War*, Toronto, 1941, p. 80.

16. James, *Wartime Economic Co-operation*, p. 32.

17. *Ibid.* p. 35.

18. Kenneth R. Wilson, "The External Background of Canada's Economic Problems," in J. D. Gibson, ed., *Canada's Economy in a*

Changing World, Toronto, 1948, pp. 16-19, 24-25.

19. H. F. Angus, "Canada's Interest in Multilateral Trade," in *ibid.*, p. 91.

20. R. A. Spencer, *Canada in World Affairs 1946-49*, Toronto, 1959, p. 236.

21. Bruce Hutchison, memorandum, 12 June, 1940, in King Papers, Vol. 19 (Black Binders).

22. James, *Wartime Economic Co-operation*, p. 392.

INDEX

Acheson, Dean 113ff., 133, 148; alien nature of, 124-5; anti-communism of, 114; on Article 2, 125ff; career of, 114ff.; difficulty in shaping policy consensus, 124; on U.S. economic power, 121-2; on effects of Korean War, 146-7; lack of idealism, 119; on NATO, 122, 125ff.; on UN, 121; on U.S. power, 121; on Canadian woolly moralizing, 123, 126-7.

Alaska Highway 108

American Cyanamid Co. 65

Anti-communism 114, 118, 133, 145ff.

Army, U.S. and Great War economic mobilization, 14

Atlantic Charter 106

Aron, Raymond 7

Balfour, Lord 28, 43

Bank of Canada 98-9, 100

Baruch, Bernard 19, 37, 45, 48, 52, 58; on business health, 17; Chairman, WIB, 14; disillusionment re WIB difficulties, 13; on government-industry relations, 16; Member Price-Fixing Committee, 14; and WIB, 12

Beck, Adam 63, 65

Berle, A.A. 99-100, 161-2

Borden, Robert 21, 22, 30, 32, 39, 44, 51, 52, 55, 60, 67, 157; agreement with Liberals 1911, 51; on Canada-U.S. cooperation, 37-8; on Canada-U.S. trade, 31; and Canadian representation in U.S., 45, 50; congratulates Harris, 56; on IMB-Ordnance Agreement, 36; on IMB Washington office, 53; on need for Canadian war mission, 54-5; and power problem, 65-6; on U.S. money market, 31; on U.S. war organization, 6; visits U.S., 37.

Bracken, John 140-1

Brand, R.H. 34-5, 48, 53, 55

Brandeis, Mr. Justice 116

British Commonwealth 111, 112

British Commonwealth Air Training Plan 72

British Forgings Co. 65

British War Mission (Washington) 34, 44, 47, 57; difficulties representing Canada, 48-9; relation with IMB in Washington, 53

Brookings, R.S. 12, 14, 17, 18

Brown and Williamson Tobacco 71

Canada; agrees to finance U.K. orders, 82; aid to U.K., 140-1; anti-communism of, 117; attitude